THE PRACTICAL GUIDE TO BUYING AND RUNNING
A SMALLHOLDING IN WALES

THE PRACTICAL GUIDE TO BUYING AND RUNNING A SMALLHOLDING IN WALES

Liz Shankland

UNIVERSITY OF WALES PRESS CARDIFF 2008

www.uwp.co.uk

British Library Cataloguing-in-Publication Data
A catalogue record for this book is available from the British Library.

ISBN 978-0-7083-2138-6

The right of Liz Shankland to be identified as author of this work has been asserted by her in accordance with sections 77 and 79 of the Copyright, Designs and Patents Act 1988.

Typeset by cbdesign
Printed in Great Britain by Henry Ling Limited, Dorset

To my dad, Bryn, a townie who loved the countryside
and who would have been thrilled about my new life.

CONTENTS

PREFACE

S OME PEOPLE thought we were mad. Many still do. Why on earth, they asked, would we want to swap our lovely, modern home on a sought-after housing development, for a 300-year-old farmhouse in need of serious renovation? Why, after putting three years' hard labour into decorating and remodelling the house and completely redesigning the garden, would we want to give everything up for some scruffy fields of unruly pasture land next door to a working farm?

They just didn't get it. And, in fairness, we understood their reaction. After all, we hadn't even been *thinking about* moving house, let alone considering a major lifestyle change. Quite simply, we couldn't explain to anyone why we were taking such a big step – but we knew it just *felt* right.

I grew up in a terraced house in Merthyr Tydfil, south Wales. Once, the town was the industrial capital of the world, famous for its iron and steel production. Now, sadly, it's an unemployment blackspot bearing all the classic scars of having been exploited during and in the wake of the industrial revolution. Our family was fortunate in that we had a back garden, lovingly tended by my mum. I got the gardening bug thanks to her and, many years later, when I started caring for gardens of my own, I began to realize that what I really yearned for was the archetypal 'house with a bit of land'.

Happily, I ended up marrying Gerry Toms, another townie who shared the same dream. What he also had was the vision and determination to convince us both that it really could happen.

Of course, it didn't help that, just as we were moving, the BBC launched its new drama series, *Down to Earth*, starring Pauline Quirke and Warren Clarke as two rat-race escapees from London throwing in their jobs and buying a smallholding in the country. Comparisons with the series – and quips about being like Tom and Barbara in the old sitcom, *The Good Life* – came thick and fast.

We let them all have their laugh. What our bemused friends were overlooking was that, unlike the TV characters, we weren't taking the plunge completely. Both of us were keeping our city-based jobs, and planning to fit our new commitments around our normal working lives – mine in the media, Gerry's in policing.

One day I would be conducting a serious interview with a politician, the next back home, hacking away at killer brambles; Gerry would unblock our primitive sewage system, then change into uniform to give a pre-match briefing to hundreds of officers about handling soccer hooligans. Our social life all but disappeared, weekend callers would invariably find us covered in mud (or worse), and we were permanently shattered – but blissfully happy.

A few years down the line, our working lives have changed somewhat. Two years after moving, Gerry retired and went into part-time consultancy work, but a tempting opportunity arose and he is now General Manager of the Millennium Stadium in Cardiff. I'm still doing the same kind of work as I've always done, but I'm doing more from home, which gives me the time and flexibility to look after my livestock.

Right now, we feel we've just about found the right balance between making the best use of our time and working ourselves to exhaustion. What's more, we've managed to convince many of the sceptics that we were right to follow our instincts and buy this place. And, judging by the number of people we've had knocking on the door, asking if we'd consider selling, it seems we're not as mad as some may have thought.

When I started writing this book, Gerry and I had absolutely no intentions of leaving our smallholding. It was all we thought we would ever want. But times, needs and preferences change, and we've recently started home-hunting again – for a place with more land for me and, if possible, a river frontage with fishing rights to keep Gerry happy. This time we'll have experience and knowledge under our belts, and we'll hopefully have a better idea of what we're looking for. At least that's the plan.

ABOUT THE AUTHOR

LIZ SHANKLAND is a journalist and broadcaster who has worked for more than twenty-five years in newspapers, TV, and radio. Born and brought up in a terraced house in Merthyr Tydfil, she has a smallholding high above Caerphilly, where she keeps rare breed pigs, sheep, chickens and turkeys.

Her career began as a cub reporter on weekly newspapers in the south Wales valleys. She later moved to dailies, working for *The News* in Portsmouth and the *South Wales Echo* in Cardiff. She worked in both news and features at the *Western Mail* before being headhunted to become a producer and director with a Welsh-language TV company.

Liz worked as a BBC Wales news journalist for several years and also contributed to the Radio Wales rural affairs series, *Country Focus*.

Now a freelance writer and broadcaster, she is a regular contributor to newspapers, magazines, and radio programmes. For the past six years she has been writing a weekly column about smallholding, 'Down to Earth', in the *Western Mail*'s 'Country and Farming' section – the column which provided the impetus for this book. She also writes each month about pigs and poultry in *Country Smallholding*, the most popular magazine with downshifters and 'good lifers'.

Liz is a keen naturalist, works with the Wildlife Trusts in Wales, and edits a magazine, *Welsh Wildlife*. She has appeared as a guest presenter on the S4C gardening programme, *Clwb Garddio*, and is frequently asked by TV and radio production teams to provide expert advice on agricultural and countryside matters.

She is married to Gerry Toms, a former Chief Superintendent with South Wales Police who now runs Cardiff's Millennium Stadium. She has a son, Josh – a musician – and three Welsh Mountain Dogs, Bryn, Stella, and Gordon.

INTRODUCTION

THE IDEA FOR THIS BOOK came largely from the readers of the *Western Mail*, one of two national daily newspapers in Wales. For the past six years, I've been writing 'Down to Earth', a weekly column in the paper's 'Country & Farming' supplement. The column began as a kind of informal diary of the various experiences – and the numerous disasters – that my husband Gerry and I encountered as we made our way as complete beginners in the mysterious world of smallholding.

Back in 2002, I managed to convince Sheila Coleman, who was then the paper's farming editor, that there was one vital element missing in the 'Country & Farming' supplement. I knew it needed something written with smaller-scale farmers in mind, but which would also be interesting and accessible to all readers – whether they had a smallholding, were still at the dreaming stage, or just enjoyed reading about the countryside. Thanks to her successor Steve Dubé, the column is still alive and kicking. It is still entertaining and infuriating folk every Tuesday and reaching readers elsewhere in the UK and in some distant, exotic parts of the world, thanks to the paper's website (*www.walesonline.co.uk*). You can read some examples in Chapter 12.

When I started the column, I had no idea quite how it would be received, but I felt there was certainly a gap that needed filling; the kind of weekly article that neither assumed too much knowledge about agriculture and the countryside, nor talked down to the reader by over-simplifying matters. On the one hand, I wanted people to realize that taking on a few acres, managing land and buildings, and caring for livestock was not as easy as the TV programmes sometimes made out. However, I also wanted them to understand that, even for someone with no experience, such a change of lifestyle was achievable – with some hard work. Above all, I wanted the column to be an enjoyable read. The philosophy Gerry and I both share is that, when things are tough, and even when things go horribly wrong, you need to be able to laugh at yourself.

Six years on, I'm flattered and somewhat amazed to be told that my weekly ramblings have become the most popular regular feature in 'C & F'. The number of letters and e-mails I get about the articles I've written certainly seem to back that up. Steve Dubé is used to readers turning up at his office in Carmarthen, west Wales, convinced they will find me there because of the contact address at the end of each column. Usually they want advice on some aspect of land or livestock management. Sometimes they want to pass on some funny anecdotes about their own experiences. Other times they feel the need to share some bizarre family secret, passed down the generations from father to son – anything from determining the sex of a chick using a needle and a bit of thread to getting your carrots to grow to prize-winning standard. Occasionally, a caller will arrive who is clearly on the warpath, furious and banging on the counter, ready to give me a piece of his or her mind – usually because I've been writing about my hatred of thieving magpies, or explaining Gerry's trial-and-error methods for combating other pests. Steve, being the gentleman he is, treats them all with the same patience and courtesy, and suggests they write a letter to pass on to me.

I wanted this book to be rather different from the standard 'how to' advice books that I've read over the years. You'll see that *The Practical Guide to Buying and Running a Smallholding in Wales* includes some case studies from people who have made the move from urban life to country life, telling their own tales – good and bad. It also includes some of my favourite columns published in the *Western Mail* – often written as a kind of release from the tension when things went wrong as Gerry and I bumbled our way along as novice smallholders.

I must say at this stage that my heartfelt thanks to go to my dear friends Grahame Davies, Phil Thomas, Nick Horton, Julian Branscombe, and Barbara Warren, who agreed to read through various parts of this book in its early stages. All experts in their particular fields, they all offered much-needed words of encouragement and advice, and – just as importantly – scrutinized the pages for inaccuracies. Gerry, of course, deserves special praise, for being so patient and understanding throughout the whole process. Lesser men would not have put up with me, I'm sure.

From a practical point of view, I hope this book will provide food for thought when you consider whether you really want to make the move from your nice, comfortable lives and give up all those things you take for granted now – a shop on the corner, cinema down the road, clean carpets, reliable central heating, and a back garden that takes care of itself as long as you drag out the lawnmower a couple of times a year.

I intended this book to be a useful guide for anyone considering buying a place with land, wherever the target location might be. However, you will see that I have devoted an entire chapter aimed at people from outside Wales thinking of settling here. A considerable number of readers who contact me through the *Western Mail* are people who have moved to Wales from other parts of the UK – most commonly the south of England – or are contemplating a move. Wales has become the new, more affordable alternative to Cornwall and Devon for many looking to buy up a piece of paradise. Despite the housing market going mad in some parts of the UK, it is still possible to buy a lovely detached home and several acres of land in many of the most beautiful parts of Wales for a fraction of the price you would expect to pay in the Home Counties.

Often the people who take the opportunity to do so end up loving Wales as much those who were born here. Others, however, find it a real culture shock. Why? Because Wales is a COUNTRY, a NATION – not a region of England. I tackle the practicalities of coming to live in Wales in detail in Chapter 2, but if you're thinking about moving here, what I would urge you to do at this stage is to do your research first and make sure that Wales is right for you. Wales may be just a few hundred miles away from where you live at the moment, but in real terms it could be a million miles from the place you want it to be.

ARE YOU READY TO LIVE THE DREAM?

CONSIDER THESE PHRASES: downshifting; escaping the rat-race; getting back to nature; living the good life. All phrases we are familiar with in the twenty-first century, and all phrases we throw into conversation when we talk about moving out of urban life and into the countryside. People become smallholders for numerous reasons. Some, like me, do it on a whim – but I wouldn't recommend it.

It was about 8.30 p.m. on Tuesday, 11 July 2000, when my particular journey into the unknown began. I had just got home after my hour-long trek from work in Bristol. Every day I left home at 6.45 a.m. to beat the traffic and get a parking space near the BBC. I was at my desk an hour before I needed to be, but it saved me a fortune at the multi-storey car park. Instead of finishing at 5 p.m., I would hang on a good hour or so and do some extra work to miss the soul-destroying traffic jams on the way back. It was a great job, but in the wrong place. I hardly saw my 10-year-old son, nor my husband Gerry, who had a hugely demanding job with South Wales Police as the Chief Superintendent in charge of the city of Cardiff.

So there I was, as usual, standing in the kitchen – tired, irritable, and idly flicking through some newspapers whilst wondering which convenience meals to pull out of the freezer for dinner. I picked up the property supplement. I've no idea why, because we weren't looking for a new house at the time. We had, in fact, spent three years renovating our 1970s time capsule of a home, which had come complete with kitchen to dining-room serving hatch, swirly Artex ceilings, brown and orange carpets, and boring, lawned gardens with predictable low-maintenance shrubs and Leylandii hedges. After so much hard graft and expense, we were going to stay put and enjoy it.

At least, that's what we thought. Normally smallholdings featured in the paper were deep in west Wales, a good hour or two from Gerry's work and our families, and even more out of the question as far as my capacity for commuting was concerned. But this time, the place that caught my eye was on the outskirts of Caerphilly, just three or four miles away. I showed it to Gerry – more out of surprise than anything else. 'I know where that place is', he said, and the next thing I knew, we were in the car and on the way there.

We climbed up a single-track road, flanked by tall hedges, and then the public highway seemed to dissolve in front of us into a rocky mountain track which looked impassable by vehicles. The only option was to turn right, into a farmyard, where we recognized the house from the picture in the paper.

We only paused a few minutes before turning the car round and heading home, but we both knew then and there that we had found something a bit special. The next morning I was on the phone to the estate agent, asking for a viewing. By Saturday we were taking a tour around the property. Later in the week, we went for another look. As we stood in the bottom fields, looking back up towards the house, we decided we had to have it. Minutes later, we offered the farmer the full asking price and he accepted.

Time to Stop and Think! Is This Really What you Want, and Can you Do it?

I wouldn't for one minute suggest that anyone followed our impetuous example. Hopefully, if you have gone as far as buying this book, you'll have at least considered some of the pros and cons of taking on a place in the country with a piece of land bigger than the average lawn. I do hope so, for your sake. Gerry and I learned by our mistakes, and our transformation from inexperienced townies to semi-competent smallholders was slow, expensive, tiring and often frustrating. We got there because were both determined, adaptable, willing to make sacrifices and, thankfully, shared a sense of humour.

In our case, we didn't really know what we wanted until we found it. True, we had always wanted a house with a bit more space between us and the neighbours; we had always enjoyed working outside together on our previous house, loving the aching satisfaction at the end of a day of good, hard labour; and we loved just sitting outside, at the end of a busy day, watching the birds flying home to their roosts and the bats flitting about overhead.

Saying all that, it took a long time for us to realize that what we really wanted was a different, slower way of life, a life which meant there was time to appreciate our surroundings. So often in this world we work all the hours God sends just to pay for expensive homes, furniture and gadgets which we never have time to enjoy. Pretty soon, we realized we were thinking of downshifting, escaping the rat-race, getting back to nature, living the good life – all those things I asked you to consider at the start of this chapter. The only stumbling block was how to do it. Our new place cost twice what we got for our old house, so there was no question of either of us giving up work. Gerry was still a few years from the all-important thirty-year landmark with the police, when he could retire on a full pension at 49. I was eleven years younger than Gerry and decades away from pensionable age. We had no alternative other than to remain full-time wage-slaves and compromise by becoming part-time smallholders, at least for a while.

Making Decisions that Involve Others

If you're living with someone who shares your dreams and ideals about moving to the countryside, you're part of the way there. If there are other people involved, it naturally gets a bit more complicated. It's no longer merely about the kind of lifestyle *you* want, but to what extent others will be able to adjust to it.

How, for example, would teenagers cope with living miles away from the kind of things they take for granted – their friends, trendy high street stores, fast food take-aways, cinemas and DVD rental shops, for example? As many smallholders who are parents will tell you, *Hell hath no fury like a teenager torn out of comfortable suburbia and sent to languish in a remote farmhouse with draughts, mice and no broadband.*

What you Think you Want and What you Think you Can Achieve

There are times when we all think we know what we want. Unfortunately, reality can be very different. Ask yourself some questions.

Would everyone in my household be happy with the idea of moving to the countryside?

It's far better to get all this out in the open before you go too far. Even your partner – however loyal and supportive – might have some nagging doubts. Depending on how far away you're moving, you might also have to consider the impact on elderly parents and other relatives who are used to seeing you. Sit down with everyone concerned, let them voice their opinions, and make a brutally honest list of all the pros and cons of moving.

Do I really want to take on a smallholding and all the responsibilities being a landowner can involve?

There could be some compromise solutions, if all you want are some elements of the smallholder lifestyle. Would you, for instance, be better off buying a rural cottage, so that you could enjoy easy access to your favourite walks, but not have the burden of looking after land or livestock? If riding is your thing, and you're thinking of a move so you can buy a horse and stable it, wouldn't renting a paddock or finding a livery yard make more sense? And here's the big one. Are you just dissatisfied with your current lifestyle – your job or your relationship, for example – and in need of some other kind of change? A smallholding might act as a temporary distraction from your problems, but there are no guarantees it will solve them.

Could I give up the convenience of living in the town or city?

Consider your shopping habits, and the thought of having to drive miles each time you run out of the essentials. Think, too, of how convenient it is to slip out for a DVD and a takeaway curry. Popping in for a drink at the nearest 'local' could well mean taking the car, so that long-awaited pint you think you deserve might have to be a pint of squash.

3

Do I have the time and the dedication to devote to a smallholding?
Land won't just look after itself. Pasture land which has been grazed with sheep or cattle is likely to be incredibly high in nutrients and, if left ungrazed, will soon become overgrown with all those weeds everyone loves to hate, like dock, nettles and creeping buttercup. Assuming you intend to continue working full-time, you're not going to have much spare time to look after your land or any livestock. You might end up renting out your fields to a neighbouring farmer – in which case the land might not really feel like your own. How might you feel about that? On the other hand, if you're determined to grow crops or raise livestock, you may have to buy in some help. Could you afford to?

If you decide that a half-way house compromise could work (like keeping your regular job whilst devoting all your spare time to your smallholding), could you honestly say you would have the energy and enthusiasm at the end of a working day to get changed and start work all over again? If you're in a relationship, or have a family, what would the others in your life think about being deprived of your time and attention?

And, what would happen if, for instance, you were to become ill, wanted a holiday or had to be away for a while because of your job? Who would take over your chores? I didn't realize the importance of having someone to step into the breach until the summer of 2007, when I fell and fractured my spine. I spent five months in a spinal brace, under strict orders to do as little as possible. Fortunately, Gerry and Josh managed between them to juggle my jobs around work and school commitments and the show went on. Had they not been in a position to be so flexible, I've no idea what we would have done.

Case Studies

Here are some of the highs and lows of buying a smallholding, as seen through the eyes of some of the contributors to the downshifters' website, *www.acountrylife.com*. Thanks to the website founder Carolyn Ekins for allowing me to include these personal accounts. Names have been changed to protect privacy.

Julie's story
It's easy to have the 'rose-tinted specs' view of smallholding. I certainly did, when I was sat in my office at my old job day dreaming everyday, and trawling the internet for inspiration and guidance. I had a vision of me and my other half, maybe working part-time, living in a country cottage with a few acres, small mortgage, living frugally, growing veg, making our own wine, cakes and bread.

In reality, we *have* found the cottage and managed to downshift a little. My other half has the part-time job so he can work on the house and land. Unfortunately, in order to make our cottage in Mid Wales habitable, I now have a new job that has longer hours, is more stressful, and less well-paid (Welsh salaries are not great). We moved here nearly 12 months ago, and we still have no heating other than a coal fire and two electric radiators, and my solid fuel Rayburn is not yet working. We have no toilet (bucket in traditional outhouse), no shower/bath, and, until recently, had only cold water. To wash, wash up, etc., I had to boil a kettle. Until we re-wired the place, that was on a gas camping stove as well! Although we have got used to living like this, it is not fun!

I haven't made any bread or cakes, as the kitchen is laughable (a camping gas stove and microwave), and the elderberry wine we tried to make went off through inexperience. We had a minor success with some veg this summer, but really only grew a few beans, some slug-ravaged spinach and a million courgettes. Hardly self-sufficiency! Our only apple tree had to be chopped down to make way for the JCBs, and we are currently living in a building site whilst waiting for the extension to be finished. I am regularly late for work, as I have to deal with problems with the builders, and I turn up with mud all over my shoes.

But, every morning when I wake up I can hear birds and sheep instead of traffic and sirens. When I finally get home from work, I can relax by a crackling fire, or sit and look at the fabulous view. I love living in a village, we have been very lucky and been made to feel part of the community straightway. I know more of my neighbours in 12 months than I did in seven years in the city.

Leslie's story

The fundamental problem with smallholding is the cost involved. It costs more to buy or rent the place than any 'normal' dwelling. Then there is the cost of equipment. Okay, you can buy fourth-hand, make do and mend, but sometimes buying new is the only way if you want to get something in time. Stock needs to be bought, nurtured, and fed before it can possibly generate a return. There are vet fees, medicines, supplements. The bureaucrats want their pound of flesh too. We found the reserves very quickly vanish. If you're not careful, I suspect a mountain of debt is very easy to accumulate against which the meagre return looks very sad.

If, of course, smallholding is purely a hobby and you have a decent job providing a 'normal' income, then it's just like any other hobby, I guess – fishing, skiing, whatever. But even then you have to consider the substantial time cost. You must keep at it, regardless of other commitments; you can't just say, 'It's raining, we won't go out', or 'We'll go to Alton Towers today'. Not only are full holidays out, but other sorts of 'time out' will be curtailed. In winter, daylight is limited and if you have jobs to do, it really is best to get them done while the light is there – so you have less opportunity for leisure.

Smallholding, and farming in general, is a way of life not experienced by most modern people. It pervades everything you do because the tasks you have to get done must come first; anything else fits around them, or is dropped until the animals are fed, fenced, and cared for. Sure, I could dwell on muck-shovelling, fixing broken fences in a snowstorm, chasing escaped animals, juggling tasks all of which need doing before each other. But the cost in money and time are the fundamental problems!

Ellie's story

The 'dream' is so much more affordable now than it ever has been. Low mortgage rates, increases in equity through rising property markets etc. Yes, a smallholding in Wales or wherever is more expensive than it was, but compared to increases in the south-east of England, it's a joke.

Why, when generations of farmers and smallholders have been unsuccessful in a venture does an IT consultant think he/she could turn it around? For a smallholding to be viable, it needs either lots of experience or investment, and there's no guarantee that either will work. If a smallholding is cheap, there's a reason – poor land, lack of access etc., all of which have a huge impact on viability. The old adage of 'buy the best you can afford' rings true here. My experience has taught me that unless the smallholding can stand on its own two feet as a business, and is debt free, I'm not doing it. As a business, I mean wholesale production of some sort – I have no interest in selling the odd thing here or there for a quid or two. It's pointless.

Keep all the organically grown/reared stuff for yourself to reduce your costs, or for a bit of beer money. The vast majority of the paying public couldn't give a stuff if it's grown here or in Kenya. And unless you are very fortunate, my opinion would be you are on a hiding to nothing if you base a business plan on a premium product in what is fast becoming an over-supplied market.

John's story

Smallholding is a lifestyle. Nothing more, nothing less. Anyone who thinks that they can live off a few acres and live the good life needs to do some serious rethinking. The TV programme, *The Good Life* – delightful as it was – did more harm than good, giving the idea that you can live off fresh air.

It is essential that you have at least one regular and substantial income because you will have to keep yourselves as well as your stock. They will not keep you. Farmers have some help with Single Farm Payment and agri-environmental schemes, but most smallholders don't have sufficient land to be able to claim.

The argument that giving up a day job will provide freedom is also erroneous as one is more tied to a smallholding than any paid employment.

As a member of a smallholders' group I see that those who have a firm financial footing, either in the form of regular employment or substantial pensions, are the most content. Those who are less well off are constantly chasing their own tails in an effort to keep their heads above water.

This may sound like the ranting of an embittered old lady but it isn't. It's the reality. I love my lifestyle, but I have the luxury of no mortgage, a pension, sufficient land to be able to claim government support payments, and diversification businesses from the farm.

Huddled around an open fire in a cold, damp cottage with no central heating and living off your garden and a few chickens may seem 'the dream' when you are not doing it but the reality is very different. You can only economize so much by growing your own veg and meat. You still have to pay for all the other things that you had to pay for before. Just add up your monthly outgoings on council tax, insurance, heating and lighting etc. to put things into perspective.

2

A WELCOME IN THE HILLSIDE?

This chapter is written primarily for the benefit of those from outside Wales who are considering a move here. Feel free to skip this section if it doesn't apply to you, or if you've decided you're going to build a moat around your property and avoid speaking to the locals. Even if you're already living in Wales, but are moving from one of the more Anglicized parts to a Welsh-speaking area, it may be of help.

WE WELSH ARE a very welcoming sort on the whole and, throughout history, Wales has continued to be a real melting-pot of cultures. That said, it must be remembered that Wales is, nevertheless, a country in its own right; it is a nation, with a population proud of its language and its identity.

In the more Anglicized parts of Wales, such as the south-east and 'little England' (southern Pembrokeshire), you will find many native Welsh people who have never spoken the language. That said, they can be as fiercely patriotic – sometimes more so – as Welsh speakers whose families have used the language for generations. Just because someone doesn't speak Welsh doesn't necessarily mean that they love their country any less.

In the more traditional Welsh-speaking areas – particularly the heartlands in parts of the north and the west – protection and encouragement of the language is a much bigger deal, and you should be aware that becoming a part of a community in these areas can be much more difficult if you don't see the point of bilingualism.

I don't want to sound as if I'm trying to say that you're not wanted here if you're not Welsh. The advice I want to pass on at this point is that you might have to do a bit more work at settling into some areas than others. It's just advice, of course, so feel free to ignore it if you wish. Just don't say I didn't warn you.

Why Should Moving to Wales be Different?

Most Welsh people will welcome you with open arms – as long as you take the time to acknowledge their country's status and make a conscious effort to fit in and become part of the local community. What I don't want anyone to do is make the move thinking everything is going to be the same as wherever they came from, and then end up disappointed.

Rule no. 1 is that you must understand that Wales is our country and we are rightly proud of it. We love the things which make it different from other countries: our culture, our language, our landscapes, and the weird and wonderful people who live here and who make it what is is.

Although we don't burn down holiday homes any more, there are still some areas where incomers (There, I've said it! Sorry, but that's what you'll be. It's not meant in a derogatory way) may not be made quite so welcome if they don't make the effort to integrate.

You'll have to get used to the idea of us having two languages of equal status, you'll need to accept that your children will go to a school where Welsh forms at least part of their education – possibly a very large part – and you'll have to acknowledge the fact that we have our own government, which occasionally chooses to do things differently to the one in Westminster.

The main plea I want to make in this section is, please don't decide to move here just because it's cheaper than other places you've considered. And don't come here expecting *us* to change to suit the way *you* want to live. We like it this way.

Who Runs Wales?

Let's start by discussing one of the great bug-bears of many incomers: the National Assembly for Wales. If you want to come here to live, you have to accept that we have our own government, and no amount of whining and moaning is going to change that. You will hear two phrases containing the word 'assembly': the Welsh Assembly Government (WAG) and the National Assembly for Wales (NAW). The WAG develops and implements policy, while the NAW debates and approves legislation and holds the Assembly Government to account. The

Constituencies of Wales (Welsh Assembly Government

relationship between the two is similar to the UK Government's relationship with the Houses of Parliament. The debating chamber, the Senedd – a glass, wood, and slate structure designed by Lord Rogers – occupies a prime spot in Cardiff Bay, the revamped docklands area of the Welsh capital, with an administration block at neighbouring Crickhowell House.

The Assembly has been here since 1999, when sixty Assembly Members (AMs) were elected. AMs are elected in two ways: forty are chosen by the first-past-the-post system – the same as in the Westminster elections – and represent the same forty geographical constituencies as the Westminster MPs; the other twenty members (known as 'regional' or 'list' members, although they have the same status as their constituency colleagues) represent five larger regions of Wales. There are four to each region, elected using a complicated form of proportional representation called the Additional Member System. The letters 'AM' ('Assembly Member') are used after a member's name, just as 'MP' is used after the name of a Member of Parliament. You may also see the letters 'AS' ('Aelod Seneddol') after a member's name in Welsh-language publications or in captions on the Welsh TV news.

The WAG is responsible for many of the things which matter to the people of Wales, including health, education, economic development, the environment, local government, social services, sport, culture, transport and the Welsh language. There are a number of important areas where it has no authority, notably policing, defence and national security, monetary policy, tax-raising, employment legislation, foreign policy, social security and broadcasting. But things could change. Plans for a referendum to set up a full Welsh Parliament, along the same lines as the Scottish model, were key to the coalition deal between Labour and Plaid Cymru after the May 2007 Assembly election. In October 2007, First Minister Rhodri Morgan announced that Sir Emyr Jones Parry, a former UK Ambassador to the United Nations, would chair a convention to test the public appetite for change. A referendum would decide whether or not the Assembly should be upgraded to the level of a full parliament with the ability to make laws. Should the new incarnation get the go-ahead, however, it is unlikely that changes will be made to a few political hot potatoes; there is not likely to be an increase in the number of members, an overhaul of the electoral system, nor an introduction of tax-raising powers.

The WAG is made up of a First Minister, ministers and deputy ministers responsible for various departments covering all the key areas of responsibility, and the Counsel General, who is the chief legal adviser to the Assembly. Full sessions of the NAW are held twice a week, on a Tuesday and Wednesday afternoon, and smaller subject committees work throughout the week. All sessions are open to the public. AMs may speak in Welsh or English, and extremely efficient simultaneous translation facilities are provided. When Wales decided it was going to elect an Assembly, sixty politicians had to be found from somewhere. Although some MPs stood in their own constituencies, many of those who entered the election were drawn from the ranks of local government. Others came from a range of backgrounds, both in the public and private sector. Consequently, few of the AMs elected had considerable political experience, and it took some time for them to find their feet.

In fairness, it is still early days. The Assembly is a young institution and needs time to grow and mature. I have no doubt it will. There have been a few significant changes for the better, like abolishing charges for prescriptions, giving free public transport and swimming lessons to pensioners, and free admission for all to museums and galleries. The Assembly also did away with university 'top-up' fees, making it significantly cheaper to study in Wales. It was the first to appoint a Children's Commissioner to protect children's rights; England, Scotland, and Northern Ireland followed suit. In a similar vein, it later created the first Older People's Commissioner. On a more controversial note, the Assembly dug its heels in during the debate over test crops of genetically modified crops, insisting that Wales remain a GM-free zone.

Welsh Attitudes to Incomers

Back in the late 1970s, the satirical BBC TV show *Not the Nine O'Clock News* ran a sketch which was a spoof of a British Coal TV advertisement. Images of roaring flames played against a soundtrack of a Welsh male voice choir and the voiceover urged, 'Come home to a real fire – buy a holiday cottage in Wales'. The sketch alluded to more than a decade of incidents which began in 1979 and involved the burning of second homes, caravans, cars, estate agents' offices and other businesses owned by English people. Responsibility for most of the incidents was claimed by a group calling itself Meibion Glyndŵr (Sons of Glyndŵr), named after Owain Glyndŵr, the celebrated patriot and self-appointed prince of Wales who led a rebellion against the English in the fifteenth century.

The violence was down to a combination of factors, principally the decline of the Welsh language (more of this later) and an increasing trend during the 1970s and 1980s towards people from outside Wales buying second homes which lay unused for a great deal of the time. As demand for holiday homes grew, so did the price of housing – with the result that properties in certain areas of Wales were pushed way out of the reach of local people.

At the same time, there was a significant increase in the number of people moving to parts of rural Wales – particularly in the north and west – from other parts of the UK. Many, it must be said, were 'good-lifers', taking the advice of the granddaddy of self-sufficiency, John Seymour, to embrace a slower, better-quality lifestyle in beautiful surroundings. For the price of a small house in the south of England, they could buy a decent farm in Wales. No change there, then.

So, as young locals were being forced to move out of their home towns and villages because of dwindling job opportunities and rising house prices, non-Welsh speakers with money in their pockets were moving in to take their place. Not surprisingly, there were feelings of unrest and insecurity and serious concerns for the future of the Welsh language in these communities where the cultural and linguistic dynamic was changing rapidly. Once again, Wales seemed to be under siege; just like centuries before, it was drowning under the tide of English incomers. No excuse for arson, though, you might argue.

Understanding the Background

You have to appreciate that the Welsh language had been taking a beating at the hands of the English since the sixteenth century, when the Acts of Union of 1536 and 1543 demoted Wales to being just another part of England and made English the official language. As if that wasn't bad enough, in 1847, three English government officials were sent to Wales to compile a report about education standards. The result – known as The Blue Books – not only concluded that education was in an appalling state, but that the Welsh were ignorant, lazy, drunken and immoral cheats. Use of the Welsh language and religious preference for Nonconformity were blamed for the problems. One way of discouraging the use of the language in schoolchildren in some schools during the eighteenth and nineteenth centuries was to a hang a small piece of wood or slate inscribed with 'WN' – which stood for 'Welsh Not' – around the neck of any child caught speaking Welsh. Every time another child spoke Welsh, the symbol of shame would be passed on and, at the end of the day, whoever was left with it was punished.

Oppression of the language persisted into the twentieth century, with Welsh having no status in business nor education. The political party Plaid Cymru (literally, 'the party of Wales') was formed in 1925, with the principal aims of saving the Welsh language from further decline and making Welsh the only official language of Wales – but with the longer term goal of self-government.

Sign of the times: this traditional Welsh church in Carmarthenshire is advertising services in English in a bid to swell its congregation.

In 1962, one of the party's founders, Saunders Lewis, issued a battle cry to protect the language in a BBC radio lecture, *Tynged yr Iaith* ('fate of the language'). 'Restoring the Welsh language in Wales is nothing less than a revolution,' he said. 'It is only through revolutionary means that we can succeed.' The lecture mourned the decline of the language, led to the birth in 1963 of Cymdeithas yr Iaith (the Welsh Language Society) and signalled the start of energetic campaigning which would continue for decades.

The first real focal point for the newly motivated Welsh nationalist movement was the creation of a reservoir, Llyn Celyn in the Tryweryn valley in north Wales. In 1965, the community of Capel Celyn, a tiny village near Bala, was destroyed; some 800 acres of land were flooded, along with the school, the post office, the chapel, the cemetery and a dozen homes and farms, in order to satisfy Liverpool City Council's demand for a new reservoir to provide water for the city. Despite objections in the House of Commons by all but one of the thirty-six Welsh MPs – and despite innumerable protests back home in Wales – the development was allowed to proceed. The Tryweryn project is often described as a catalyst event in the campaign for Welsh independence. Demonstrations continued through its construction, attempts were made to sabotage works and furious opponents did their best to wreck the opening ceremony.

The investiture of the Queen's eldest son as Prince of Wales in Caernarfon in 1969 aroused further anti-English hostility and provided another impetus for protests. The campaign against the investiture culminated when two members of Mudiad Amddiffyn Cymru (Welsh Defence Movement) tried to derail Prince Charles's train and stop it reaching Caernarfon. Alwyn Jones and George Taylor were killed when the bomb they had planned to place on the railway line at Abergele exploded unexpectedly.

The years which followed would see many extreme examples of nationalistic protest like the Abergele incident. However, it must be pointed out that it wasn't all bombings and arson attacks. The majority of the events orchestrated in the campaign for independence and the survival of the language were non-violent.

Conflict in the Twenty-first Century

The fight to protect the Welsh language and culture and to preserve traditionally Welsh-speaking communities may have lost its aggression in recent years, but the sentiments behind the protest are as strong as ever. Most vocal in the field has been Cymuned (Community), which describes itself as a 'Welsh-language civil rights movement'.

Since being formed in 2001, the group has made repeated calls for local people to be given help to buy homes in their own communities. The organization also wants action to be taken to address the problem of people moving into Wales but refusing to learn the language. American academic Dr Jerry Hunter is a member of Cymuned. He has learned the language and lectures in Welsh at Bangor University. He lives in a Welsh-speaking community in the Nantlle Valley in Gwynedd and, as someone who is neither

Welsh nor English, speaks with a multi-faceted view of the language debate. He says on the organization's website, *www.cymuned.net*:

> We welcome the in-migration of individuals from non-Welsh backgrounds into Wales who learn the Welsh language and contribute to cultural and social life: we believe that they add to the diversity of experiences that exist in Wales, but we do not believe that an influx into our communities of individuals who refuse to respect the existence of a minority culture is conducive to social justice, multi-culturalism or linguistic diversity.

Half-English, half-Welsh Jan Morris has written passionately and extensively about Wales and the Welsh identity. In an article titled, 'Go Home, Englishman', she laments the way some English settlers choose to ignore the fact that Wales has its own, living language, and identity:

> Yes, everyone can speak English and the Welsh, being a courteous race, all too anxious to please, will readily use English to converse with strangers. Superficially the newcomer will soon be at home. The laws are more or less the same, after all. The supermarkets sell Pot Noodles and crisps. The neighbours are mostly kindly. You don't have to watch Welsh-language television. It's not like going to the Eisteddfod! Except that it *ought* to be like going to the Eisteddfod. All too many of those English incomers will remain entirely heedless of the fact that they have settled in a land where a language they do not understand is being spoken, written, gossiped and prayed in all around them, as it has been for many centuries . . . In village after village Welsh-speaking people are finding themselves in a minority, and their community is withering. When patriots object, they are branded as racists, but this is not a racist issue at all. It is a question of cultural survival, it stands above race or even nationality. (*The Spectator*, 31 August 2002)

I like to think that people from outside Wales are becoming less Cymraeg-phobic but, every so often, something happens to knock that theory on the head. The most recent was a front-page article in the *Sunday Telegraph* (15 January 2008) in which Clive Aslet from *Country Life* magazine took a look at some of the 'bargain' smallholdings (costing up to £1.25m) on offer in Wales.

Predictably, there were all the usual kind of smug London hack observations: imagery like 'broad-shouldered mountains gather round you like a gigantic rugby scrum'; a comment about a property being 'reassuringly near the Herefordshire border'; and then the tired and hackneyed jibe about 'indecipherable place names'. I was half expecting him to come out with the line from the comedy series *Blackadder*, where Rowan Atkinson's eponymous hero retorts: 'If you ask for directions in Wales, you'll have to wash the spit out of your hair.'

Aslet interviewed a couple – an Australian and his German countess wife – selling their 90-acre rural retreat, which was on the market for a cool £950,000. They gave their children's education as the reason for wanting to move (Aslet comments: 'It daunts some newcomers to find that the Welsh language is a compulsory subject in all state schools in Wales, and that some of the best teach only in Welsh'). I wonder, though, whether perhaps they had never really settled in the first place. After all, they say the reason they ended up in Wales was because they couldn't find a similar property – and the 'tranquillity and privacy' they wanted – in England. 'We were in Suffolk for a year, but it was too crowded,' the husband said. Not surprisingly, the first thing they did was to change the name of the house from the rather charming and descriptive 'Cwm Creigiau Fach' ('valley of the small rocks') to 'Rivendell' – the kind of name you see on one of those soulless executive-style estates where all the houses are detached, but only by about four inches. Still, they probably had to change the name because they couldn't pronounce it – and what would have been the point in learning to say it, if they were only planning to stay a few years?

Mike Parker is an Englishman living in Ceredigion who learned Welsh and has become positively evangelical about the language. In his book, *Neighbours from Hell? English Attitudes to the Welsh* (Y Lolfa, 2007) he explains this bizarre need to Anglicize Welsh names:

> Because place and house names are often some people's only contact with the Welsh language, it's not surprising that these have become a lightning conductor for the most determined of anti-Welsh bigots in our midst ... Welsh names, that often are so beautifully descriptive and poetic, names that have survived hundreds of years in many cases, get unceremoniously chucked into the bin, and the houses are re-christened Mountain View, or named (as a property near me has been) after their egomaniac owners.

You have to appreciate that some Welsh people will get extremely annoyed if their new neighbours appear not to want to make the effort. Here are just two comments from regular users of *www.acountrylife.com*, the smallholders' website:

Lyn, Carmarthenshire

If incomers and visitors could just get their tongues around the 'll' and 'dd', remember that 'w' and 'y' are vowels, that there are no silent letters, and that generally the emphasis is placed on the last syllable but one, they should be able to at least pronounce any Welsh words or place names, even if they don't know their meanings.

Welsh is completely phonetic and such a beautiful descriptive language. It surely can't be more difficult to learn than English with its double meanings, silent letters, and irregularities – and think how many foreigners learn to speak English fluently. When in Rome and all that.

15

Margaret, Powys
I have to confess that it more than slightly irritates me that there are some people who move to Wales and don't even learn to pronounce their own address. We have neighbours in the village who have lived here eight years or so. They seem to take pride in not even *trying* to pronounce Welsh words. When this even includes their next-door neighbour's name – which they must have *heard* first, rather than read. It seems more than irritating – it is just plain rude.

So there you have it: if you're moving to a traditionally Welsh-speaking area, make the effort to acknowledge and accept the language and you'll be thanked for it; ignore or even ridicule it, and settling in might be more difficult than you imagined.

A Living Language and Culture

Welsh is one of the oldest living European languages. Written records show that the language was in use in the sixth century, but it was in use at least 1,000 years earlier. Not only is it still around, it is distinct from other languages in that it is being used every day, by 582,368 people – some 20.8 per cent of the population – and has equal status to English.

The Welsh Language Act, 1967, was the first step towards equal status, granting the right for Welsh to be used in court, and in public administration. However, it wasn't until the Welsh Language Act, 1993, that the language was put on an equal par with English in all aspects of public life. In short, it made three significant changes: it obliged the public sector – including local authorities, health trusts and government agencies – to treat Welsh and English with equal importance, which meant compulsory bilingual services and communications for the first time; it reiterated the right for Welsh to be spoken in court proceedings; and it established Bwrdd yr Iaith Gymraeg (the Welsh Language Board), a publicly funded body, to monitor the new obligations, and to generally promote and encourage the use of Welsh.

The most recent data available on the number of Welsh speakers comes from the 2001 Census, details of which were released in 2003. While the total percentage of Welsh speakers rising to 20.8 per cent was good news in itself, it was the increase with regard to the younger generation which most raised the hopes of guardians of the language. For the third consecutive time, there was an increase in the number of young Welsh speakers – more than 26 per cent of people in Wales under the age of 35 could speak the language, an increase of almost 9 per cent on the 1991 figures. In addition, more than 28 per cent of the whole population said they were able to understand Welsh, even if they didn't speak it well enough to regard themselves as fluent. The Census also revealed that although 25 per cent of people living in Wales were born elsewhere, 9 per cent of these people said they could speak Welsh.

Mike Parker reckons Wales has been waiting far too long for its original mother tongue to be recognized as equal in status to English:

> Many people waste no time in moaning like stuck pigs that the Welsh language is forced on them, or that too much money is wasted on promoting it. If, however, with the benefit of a bit of historical perspective, we just compare these pro-Welsh policies, which have only been in place for 20 years or so, with the hundreds and hundreds of years of brutal, official suppression of the language, then it becomes abundantly clear that some sort of recent redressing of the balance (or, rather, imbalance) is not only hugely overdue and desirable, but actually far less than it could, and perhaps should, be.

Welsh in the Modern World

The decline of Welsh can be traced back to the 1500s, when the Acts of Union ensured that the language would not be used as an official language again until after the passing of the 1942 Welsh Courts Act. The Acts of Union made Wales part of England, so English became the official language of business and administration here. The language was not banned, but it was significantly demoted. What followed were centuries of steady linguistic decline.

At the beginning of the twentieth century, Welsh was spoken by almost half the people in Wales. Close on one million people were recorded as Welsh speakers in the 1911 Census. In the decades that followed, numbers dwindled steadily. The reasons often quoted for this include migration from rural to urban areas; inward migration of English speakers into previously all-Welsh areas; a growth in English-language media outlets; and a slump in the popularity of religion, which led to a decline in the numbers attending chapels, which were among the mainstays of the language.

The situation became so serious that, by 1991, although it was encouraging that 508,098 people could speak Welsh, they represented just 18.7 per cent of the population. The 2001 Census results, therefore, came as a welcome boost, reinforcing hopes for the future. Although Gwynedd in

The counties of Wales

17

the north has the highest *percentage* of Welsh speakers, at 69.0 per cent (77,846), Carmarthenshire in the west has the highest *number*, with 84,196 (50.3 per cent) of the population speaking Welsh. Traditionally, south-west Wales, the north-west, and mid-Wales have had the highest percentages of Welsh speakers, but Welsh is on the increase in many urban areas not previously thought of as strongholds of the language. Cardiff – the local authority area with the largest population – saw the most significant increase in Welsh speakers; the number rose by 14,415 (4.4 per cent) to 32,504 (11 per cent of residents). Demand for Welsh-medium schools in the county is growing significantly and the city is home not only to the Welsh Assembly Government, but also to an increasing number of public sector bodies operating bilingually. Media organizations – many producing TV programmes in Welsh for S4C – are also firmly entrenched in the city.

Interestingly, 5,536 (1 per cent) of Welsh speakers come from what the Census called 'non-white ethnic groups'. These were broken down into four groups: mixed 2,910; Asian/British Asian 1,648; Black/British Black 443; and Chinese or other ethnic groups 535. The Welsh Assembly Government has launched a national action plan for a bilingual Wales, *Iaith Pawb* (Everyone's Language). Its aims include increasing the proportion of Welsh speakers by 5 per cent by 2011 and halting the decline in heartland communities, particularly those with around 70 per cent Welsh speakers. It also plans to boost the number of children in pre-school Welsh education, and increase the number of families where Welsh is the principal language.

Learning Welsh

There is absolutely nothing obliging you to learn Welsh, but you're bound to get more out of living in Wales if you do. It will be a challenge, but there is a huge amount of help and advice available for learners – much of it free. Another big advantage is that you will have the benefit of being able to hear Welsh being spoken around you. S4C (Sianel Pedwar Cymru – Channel Four Wales) provides more than eighty hours of Welsh-language programming a week via its terrestrial and digital services – much of it subtitled. There are several independent radio stations broadcasting in Welsh, as well as a national Welsh radio station, Radio Cymru, which broadcasts about 126 hours a week.

I was fortunate that my dad and my maternal grandmother spoke Welsh. Dad's family came from Dowlais Top in Merthyr, which used to be a very Welsh-speaking area, despite being at the heart of the iron and steel-making industry and attracting workers from right across the UK and even other parts of Europe. Mum, on the other hand, was brought up at the other end of town, in Georgetown and, even though her parents spoke Welsh, English was the language of the home and her school, and she never learned more than a few words.

Nan only really felt comfortable speaking Welsh, and sometimes struggled to find the correct English words. She used to look after myself and my brother when my parents were at work and we grew up understanding quite a lot of Welsh. Then, when we reached primary school age, what had always been so familiar began to disappear. Growing up in the 1960s in Merthyr, Welsh wasn't considered very important and Welsh-medium schools in the south-east were scarce. In those days, it was unheard of to send your child on a long bus ride to school. Consequently, myself and my three brothers were all educated at English-medium schools; only when we reached secondary school was Welsh introduced, and then as a second language.

Unlike my brothers, I enjoyed Welsh and was good at it, thanks to my two excellent teachers, the late Gomer Williams and Peter Griffiths (the actor Ioan Gruffudd's dad). I would have taken it to A level, had it not clashed with another subject. I tried to keep it up as best I could after leaving school but, as happens with any language when you stop using it on a regular basis, I soon got rusty and my vocabulary started to dry up. Going away to work in Portsmouth for a year didn't help, either. It wasn't until I had my son, Josh, at the age of 27, that I made a commitment to relearn what I'd forgotten.

By the time Josh was at nursery, I was pretty good – so much so that I was offered a great job working full-time through the medium of Welsh. I spent the next six years producing and directing TV features for a magazine programme, *Heno*, shown five nights a week on S4C.

Little Josh is now a strapping, 6ft-tall 18-year-old, as patriotic as they come, and proud to be bilingual. And me? I'm delighted at the way he's turned out, and I'm thoroughly pleased that I achieved my target – fluency. Learning never stops, of course, and I've recently enrolled at the University of Wales, Lampeter, on an online Welsh Studies degree course, partly to polish my Welsh writing skills. I know people argue you don't have to speak Welsh to be truly Welsh, but for me it was the final piece of the jigsaw. Since mastering the language, I feel complete.

It really annoys me when I hear non-Welsh speakers excusing themselves with that tired old phrase: 'I wish I could speak Welsh, but I wasn't lucky enough to have a Welsh education.' The point is, it can be done. I did it. Thousands of people have done it, and many more are in the process of doing it. All you need is to want to do it and to be prepared to get up off your arse, find yourself a class and work at it. It would be nice if you could learn Welsh by osmosis; the sad reality is that it does require work. But it's worth it – trust me.

Getting Started

Whatever your level, there are plenty of classes available, as well as books, CDs, DVDs and online learning facilities. Practically every college and university in Wales provides courses for adult learners, and you will find many more run in pubs, village halls and other convenient places. A good starting point is the Welsh for Adults Information Line which will give you guidance on where to look for courses. Ring 0871 23000170 or e-mail *iaith@galw.org*. Bwrdd yr Iaith Gymraeg has a comprehensive booklet called *All you Need to Know about Learning Welsh (But were Too Afraid to Ask)*, which contains just what the title suggests. It is available free by ringing 029 20878000 or by sending an e-mail to *addysg@bwrdd-yr-iaith.org.uk*

Another really useful resource is the Acen Language Centre website (*www.dysgwr.com*) which contains more than 1,000 hours of online courses and other helpful stuff. There is a mentor service and a forum where you can chat with other learners. There is a fee involved – starting at £50 for three months – and grants are available for those on low incomes.

The website is particularly useful if, for instance, you want to start learning Welsh before you move, if you prefer to study in private rather than attending for a class, or if work or other commitments get in the way of regular tuition. You can also listen online to Radio Acen FM (*www.radioacen.fm*) and there are links to even more Welsh-learning resources. In the Radio Acen shop, you can buy gifts including gift tokens for one to three hours' tuition by phone or e-mail.

A number of universities and colleges provide online correspondence courses, including the University of Glamorgan (tel. 01443 482575, or see *www.glam.ac.uk/welshpages*) and the University of Lampeter (tel. 01570 424754 or see the website *www.e-addysg.com/english*). Coleg Menai runs an online course called 'Clic-Clic-Cymraeg' on its website (*www.menai.ac.uk/clicclic*).

The broadcaster S4C has its own site for learners, *www.learnons4c.co.uk*, which has tests to help you assess your progress, an 'idiom of the day' facility and a really good section about landmarks in Welsh history, written in a snappy, easy-to-digest newspaper style. You can also download subtitles to S4C programmes after transmission. The main site (*www.s4c.co.uk*) gives listings of all the channel's programmes as well as lots of other useful information.

BBC Wales's Welsh-language online news service, *Cymru'r Byd* (*news.bbc.co.uk/welsh/* note, no 'www' prefix), is a good place to visit to improve your skills once you've started learning. It has a clever service called Vocab, which allows you to highlight a particular word in a story and see the English translation.

The BBC Wales website also has a section called *Living in Wales* (*www.bbc.co.uk/wales/livinginwales/*), where you'll find a whole collection of interesting topics, including Welsh history and politics, plus a guide for people moving to Wales which gives a taste of the language. It has an audio guide to pronunciation and lots of links to help you learn the language and settle in Wales.

Intensive Courses

One of the most popular and effective ways of learning Welsh quickly is by spending several hours a week on one of the Wlpan courses. These are run in all parts of Wales, so it should be fairly easy to find one near you. Call the Welsh for Adults Information Line for help. Some courses involve a few hours' tuition every day – perhaps before or after work – which help you to keep in the swing of things and to avoid the problem that students only studying once a week often have of starting 'cold' each lesson.

A great way to speed up learning, or to kick-start the skills you already have, is to go for the 'total immersion' route. A residential course is a way of blocking out the outside world and its distractions and concentrating on your language. The organizations mentioned earlier will be able to point you in the right direction. The Welsh Language and Heritage Centre at Nant Gwrtheyrn in Gwynedd is unique, being the only venue which offers all-year-round courses at all levels. For availability see the website (*www.nantgwrtheyrn.org*) or ring 01758 750334.

Welsh Place Names and their Meanings

To those who don't speak Welsh, place names can look incredibly scary. Even people who live in Wales but don't speak the language can feel intimidated by them. My late husband, a press photographer, hated having to try and get his tongue around the names of many of the towns and villages he was sent to on assignments. Although Welsh by birth, he never learned the language; his father was killed at sea during the Second World War, so both he and his brother were sent to a public school in Berkshire, at the expense of the Royal Navy. I remember spotting a beautiful house for sale in a street in Merthyr called Gwernllwyn Uchaf (upper alder grove). As soon as I mentioned it, he declared: 'There is no way I'm moving to a place I can't pronounce!' And that, as they say, was that. We didn't buy it.

Place names often describe the geographical surroundings or refer to the history of the area and can provide some useful information if you are searching for a smallholding. If you're pushed for time and you're wading through piles of estate agents' details, knowing a bit about Welsh words might actually help you whittle down your choice. If, for example, the name of the farm is 'Pen y Dre' (top of the town), you can expect it to be pretty high up – maybe even on a hill overlooking the town. Similarly, 'Sŵn yr Afon' (sound of the river) suggests the property is probably pretty near running water – a good or a bad thing, depending on your point of view. Of course, you might find that the name is a modern addition, totally inappropriate for the location, having been imposed by someone who saw it on a cottage miles away and just liked the sound of it!

Incidentally, if you would like to give your new property a Welsh name, take a look at *www.bbc.co.uk/wales/livinginwales/* and you'll find a handy little device which allows you to create a Welsh name for your house by inserting key features (a colour or a location, for instance), and then teaches you how to pronounce it. Genius.

The Education System

If you are moving to Wales with school-age children, Welsh is going to be a part of their lives. Depending on where you choose to live, it could be a very big part. Unless you choose to send your children to one of the few private schools in Wales, their education will either be mainly in Welsh, or Welsh will be taught as a second language. You may have a choice in the matter, but it depends on geography.

The National Assembly took control of the education system when it was created in 1999. At the same time, Welsh became a compulsory subject for all pupils, from the ages of five to sixteen. If your child attends a Welsh-medium school, most subjects will be taught through Welsh or bilingually. English is introduced at the age of seven for children from Welsh-speaking homes and results have shown that their speaking, reading and writing skills develop quickly.

Welsh-medium education is considered to be the major factor in halting and turning around almost a century of decline in the language. Demand is now so great that parents often have to register their children with a school long before they are due to start. Friends of mine living in Cardiff – which has thirteen Welsh-medium primaries, two Welsh-medium secondaries and more of both on the way – went to register their baby with the nearest Welsh-medium school within a few weeks of her birth. They were too late, and had to opt for one further away. A couple they knew had been warned of the shortage of places and had gone to the trouble of getting their child pencilled in for a place even before it was born!

Demand for Welsh-medium education is increasing like never before. It is now widely recognized that bilingualism is a good thing. Bilingual children have been shown to do better in school than monoglot pupils, and research from the United States, Canada, the Basque country, Catalonia – as well as Wales – has shown that they perform better in examinations and other tests (even when the subject is English). Learning a third language is also easier for those who are already bilingual.

When it comes to choosing a career, being bilingual can really make a difference. With so many organizations in Wales adopting bilingual policies, the opportunities for Welsh speakers are greater than ever. Even if your children don't end up working through the medium of Welsh, the fact that they can speak it will be recognized and valued by many employers here. Most local authorities in what are described as the 'heartland' areas will provide additional help for children who need extra assistance getting used to a Welsh education. Some have language centres where pupils can be taught for a few months before joining their Welsh medium school.

Pre-school teaching in Welsh is provided in the main by Mudiad Ysgolion Meithrin, the Welsh-medium nursery movement. There are hundreds of pre-school playgroups and parent and toddler groups: Cylchoedd Ti a Fi for children from 6 months old to school age, and nursery groups, Cylchoedd Meithrin, for children aged 2 and a half and over. Children from English-speaking homes rarely suffer academically when sent to Welsh-medium schools. Lots of my friends discounted Welsh-medium education because they didn't speak Welsh and were worried they wouldn't be able to help their children with homework. What a lot of rubbish! In my son's year at primary school, only two pupils had a parent who could speak Welsh – and I was one of them. I can honestly say that Josh's school results didn't indicate that he had an unfair advantage. In fact, he was frequently out-performed by many of his classmates. Saying that, however, he took to Welsh like a duck to water. He started at *meithrin* at the age of three and his progress was fascinating and incredibly satisfying to watch. Josh's late father couldn't speak the language, and when Josh was at my parents' house, English was always used, even though my dad could have talked to him in Welsh.

The Diversity of Welsh Culture

It's not all male-voice choirs, you know. Wales has turned out some of the great entertainers of the world, and is showing no sign of letting up just yet. Singers like Tom Jones, Dame Shirley Bassey, Sir Harry Secombe and, more recently, Charlotte Church and Katherine Jenkins have helped put Wales on the musical map. Bands like the Stereophonics, Manic Street Preachers, Catatonia and Super Furry Animals found international fame in the late 1990s, bringing a fresher and more modern image to the Welsh music scene. The phrase 'Cool Cymru' was born; suddenly, it was fashionable to come from Wales.

Cardiff has some excellent concert venues, the biggest being the Millennium Stadium. Although thought of by many as first and foremost a sports venue – and, of course, the home of Welsh rugby – the 74,500-seater stadium is incredibly versatile. It has hosted performances by artists including the Rolling Stones, U2, Red Hot Chili Peppers, Bon Jovi, Bruce Springsteen, Madonna, The Police and Robbie Williams. It also held the Tsunami Relief Cardiff concert in 2005, with Eric Clapton headlining. One of the features which makes the stadium so attractive to promoters of major events is the retractable roof, which means that no event is ever a washout because of bad weather.

The Wales Millennium Centre attracts a different type of audience. Sitting in the heart of Cardiff Bay, it is a centre for the performing arts and concentrates on opera, ballet, dance, musicals and comedy. It has seven resident arts companies, including the Welsh National Opera and Diversions dance company, and is also the headquarters of Urdd Gobaith Cymru, a Welsh-medium youth movement.

Discovering Eisteddfodau

An eisteddfod is a festival of music, literature and performance. The most important eisteddfod of all is the National Eisteddfod of Wales, the largest festival of competitive music and poetry in Europe. Held every year in the first week of August, the eight-day event alternates between the north and the south, and features competitions and performances entirely in Welsh.

The site of the eisteddfod is known as the *maes* ('field') and, because so much land is needed for the 150,000 or so visitors to park, it is usually on farmland or some other out-of-town location. A vast 3,500-seater pavilion is erected as the main performance area and this is where the highlights of the week, the ceremonies surrounding the chairing and crowning of the bard and the presentation of the prose medal, are held. Around the pavilion there are hundreds of other tents and stands, many hosting performances, others occupied by Welsh public- and private-sector organizations, and still more by traders selling anything from jewellery and wellies to furniture and works of art.

Other eisteddfodau include the Urdd Eisteddfod, organized by Urdd Gobaith Cymru, Wales's largest youth movement, and the International Eisteddfod, which is held in Llangollen and attracts performers from across the world. I always think an eisteddfod is a bit like Marmite: one of those love or hate things. My friend Elin loves them – so much so that, for years, she has taken time off work and trekked to wherever the National Eisteddfod is being held, just to work as one of the vast army of volunteer stewards. Personally, I'm not a fan. My experiences of eisteddfodau are of trudging through mud in the pouring rain to a soundtrack of dreary music being played through fuzzy speakers. But that's because I've never really been involved; it was never part of my upbringing.

For many Welsh families, competing at eisteddfodau, or going to watch others perform, is part of life. Just as farming folk treat the Royal Welsh Agricultural Show as their annual holiday, so thousands of Welsh speakers up sticks, pack their tents and head to

For some Welsh people eisteddffoddau are an essential part of their family history.

the campsite for the week. It is a chance to celebrate not only culture, but Welshness itself.

What I do like is the slightly weird, druidic element, with the circle of stones, the Order of the Gorsedd, whose members dress in monk-like robes of white, blue or green, according to rank, and the all-powerful Archdruid dressed in an outfit which would make the Pope look under-dressed. The ritualistic chairing and crowning ceremonies, along with the presentation of the prose medal, are definitely worth taking a look at if you like pomp and pageant. If you can't make it in person, everything is shown on S4C. If you're outside Wales but have digital TV, you can watch it on S4C Digidol, so there's really no reason to miss out.

Think About It

I know it's a lot to take in, but do consider what I've said about how learning a little about Wales, the Welsh, and the language and culture could make a big difference to your move to Wales.

- At least try learning Welsh – give it a go; ask your Welsh-speaking neighbours for help.
- Start watching S4C – most programmes are subtitled – and listening to BBC Radio Cymru and the various independent Welsh-language stations.
- Find out more about the history of Wales, to understand where we're coming from and why we're so hung up on some things.
- Keep your Welsh house name – find out what it means and how to pronounce it. Choose one if you haven't got one.
- Don't listen to incomers' myths about prejudice against the English – meet the locals and decide for yourself.
- Get involved with your new community and become a useful part of it.

RECOMMENDED READING

Colin Baker, *A Parents and Teachers Guide to Bilingualism*, Multilingual Matters, 2007
Una Cunningham-Andersson and Staffan Andersson, *Growing up with Two Languages: A Practical Guide*, Routledge, 2004
Janet Davies, *The Welsh Language*, University of Wales Press, 2005
John Davies, *A History of Wales*, Penguin, 2007
John Davies, Nigel Jenkins, Menna Baines and Peredur Lynch, *The Welsh Academy Encyclopaedia of Wales*, University of Wales Press, 2008
Gwynfor Evans, *Land of My Fathers: 2000 Years of Welsh History*, Y Lolfa, 1992
Tony Leaver, *Pronouncing Welsh Place Names*, Gwasg Carreg Gwalch, 1998
Jan Morris, *Wales: Epic Views of a Small Country*, Penguin, 2000

Mike Parker, *Neighbours from Hell? English Attitudes to the Welsh*, Y Lolfa, 2007
Carol WIlliams, *What's the Word for ... ? Beth yw'r gair am ... ?* University of Wales Press, 2004
Hywel Wyn Owen, *A Pocket Guide to the Place Names of Wales*, University of Wales Press, 2000

Useful Contacts

Acen Language Services, Tŷ Ifor, Bridge Street, Cardiff, CF10 2EE; tel. 029 20300800
(*www.acen.co.uk*)
Merched y Wawr , Stryd yr Efail, Aberystwyth, SY23 1JH; tel. 01970 611661
(*www.merchedywawr.com*)
Mudiad Ysgolion Meithrin , 145 Albany Road, Roath, Cardiff, CF24 3NT; tel. 02920436800
(*www.mym.co.uk*)
National Eisteddfod of Wales, 40 Parc Tŷ Glas, Llanishen, Cardiff, CF4 5WU; tel. 029 20763777
(*www.eisteddfod.org.uk*)
S4C, Parc Tŷ Glas, Llanishen, Cardiff, CF14 5DU; tel. 0870 600 4141 (*www.s4c.co.uk*)
Urdd Gobaith Cymru, Ffordd Llanbadarn, Aberystwyth, SY23 IEN; tel. 01970 613100
(*www.urdd.org*)
Welsh Assembly Government, Cardiff Bay, CF99 1NA; tel. 029 20825111 (*www.wales.gov.uk*)
Welsh Language Board, Yr Hen Argraffdy, Ffordd Santes Helen, Caernarfon, Gwynedd, LL55 2YD;
tel. 01286 684700l (*movingtowales@bwrdd-yr-iaith.org.uk*)
Young Farmers' Clubs, YFC Centre, Llanelwedd, Builth Wells, Powys, LD2 3NJ; tel. 01982 553502
(*www.yfc-wales.org.uk*)

3

MAKING IT WORK

O K, SO THERE'S no persuading you to forget the whole thing. You're sold on the idea, you've persuaded or bribed your loved ones, you've worked out exactly what you want out of your new home, and roughly where you want it to be. Now there's just the small matter of money.

Oh, if only it didn't matter! Of course, for some people selling up in wealthier parts of the UK, there might not be too much of a problem. If you can manage to pay off your mortgage and buy without taking out another one, all the better. That's what I'd be aiming to do next time round.

For the purpose of this exercise, however, let's assume you're going to have to borrow money to buy your smallholding, and that you and/or your partner are going to have to continue working to pay the mortgage and all the other bills. Just how is it going to work? Let's look at some of the options for you and/or your partner:

■ Keep your old job and the same income and commute
  Drawbacks: potentially a long, costly journey at either end of the day, plus more to do on the smallholding when you get home.

■ Try and find work in your new location
  Drawbacks: some skills are not easily portable, and there may not be a demand for what you have to offer in the area you have chosen; your dream home may be cheap because good jobs are scarce and wages are low.

■ Switch to working from home. This might involve freelancing, doing the same kind of work as you've always done, or setting up a new business – possibly making money from a hobby or a particular skill
  Drawbacks: working from home might not be an option, because of the type of work you do; becoming self-employed can be a daunting and complicated

prospect; demand for your work might fluctuate, as would your income; working from home requires discipline and dedication; you may need to spend money and carry out building work to create an office or workshop, and you may need planning permission; if you're used to working with others, you may not work as well in isolation.

- Try and make money out of your smallholding, selling your own produce
  Drawbacks: ask any farmer about the state of the rural economy; you will have to have land management or livestock handling skills, or be willing to acquire some; you will have to find markets for your produce or have visitors calling at your farm shop; farming can be extremely physically demanding, with long hours in cold, wet and miserable conditions; if you keep livestock, you'll have to be prepared for dealing with sickness and death, and you may even have to learn to kill in case of an emergency.

- Buy an existing rural business as a going concern
  Drawbacks: as in setting out to make money from your smallholding, economic prospects in the countryside are bleak, unless you find a real niche market; if it's not the type of work you're familiar with, or a business you know is successful, you could be buying yourself into trouble.

- Either you or your partner tries one of the above, maybe with one or other of you spending part of the week away from home
  Drawbacks: you're almost certain to suffer a drop in income; one or other of you may feel resentful because one of you is compromising more than the other.

Making Sacrifices

As I explained earlier, Gerry and I were fortunate that our new place was just a few miles away from where we lived, so logistically it wasn't a big deal. Fortunately, being a journalist, my skills were portable. Thanks to Geoff Williams, then News Editor at BBC Radio Wales, I managed to get a transfer from Bristol to Cardiff just a few weeks before we moved.

With hindsight, the logical thing to do would have been to wait the few years until Gerry retired, so that financially we were in a better position. We should have turned our backs on the farmhouse and told ourselves that we would start our search afresh when the time was right. But, as you will have gathered by now, we made our decision with our hearts, rather than our heads. We wanted that smallholding, we bought it and we promised one another we would live with the consequences. We did the sums, borrowed the money we needed and solemnly agreed we would do everything we possibly could to tighten our belts for the foreseeable future.

Whereas we had always enjoyed two or three foreign holidays a year, we did without; it was three years after moving in before we got on a plane together again. We stopped spending so much on clothes, too. I still had a wardrobe full of designer suits, from Jasper Conran to Yves St Laurent, but once we got stuck into the whole business of getting our smallholding the way we wanted it, the only labels I saw on a regular basis were the ones on my Dickies waterproof trousers and my Dunlop steel-toecapped wellies. Eating out had been something we had more or less taken for granted, and we would frequently go off to an evening do in Cardiff and stay overnight at a nice hotel rather than get a taxi back. All that stopped, too.

We even started cooking 'proper' food more often. One of my money-saving ideas was to spend less on convenience foods and to devote more time to planning our meals, buying good quality ingredients and cooking dishes from scratch. One of the things which helped was that an ancient Aga came with the house, changing forever our whole approach to cooking. Roasted joints of locally sourced meat, slow-cook casseroles and wholesome stews became the basis of our diet, all supplemented by our own vegetables. The only drawback was, I couldn't quite get the hang of baking in it (see the November column in Chapter 12), so the dogs got a lot to eat. Also, because the Aga doesn't allow any cooking smells out, countless meals were forgotten and reduced to charcoal.

Our new lifestyle was different – frugal, I suppose, in many people's eyes – but the funny thing was, we didn't really miss any of the things we gave up. The thrill of moving in and planning out the future overshadowed everything else. We hardly had a social life any more, but then we didn't have the time for one. Every spare minute we had went on renovating the house, taming the overgrown land and diverting streams which had turned the fields in front of the house into a mudbath. And we loved it. At the end of the day, we ached so much that, once we sat down, we wouldn't be able to move. But it was great – and, come to think of it, it still is.

Financial Planning

Dreaming is all very well, but getting the finances sorted before you take the plunge is a must for any would-be smallholder. What you have to do, above all else, is to make sure you can afford what you are getting into. I have always hated anything to do with money, and Gerry still has to force me to look at bank statements. I think it's something to do with an almost pathological fear of numbers. I was terrified of maths lessons as a child. I got a D grade at O level, and then actually went *down* a grade with each subsequent resit. I still have nightmares about being back in the maths class, unable to make head nor tail of the work on the board.

It's not just dreams that bother me. When I'm out shopping, I hardly ever use cash because I'm terrified of not having enough money in my purse to pay at the checkout. If I do pay cash, I have to be sure I have lots of big notes in my purse, just in case.

Inevitably, I end up with a load of loose change at the end of each day – simply because I can't trust my own ability to hand over the right amount in coins.

Nevertheless, there comes a time when we all have to confront our demons. When we decided we were going to buy our new place, Gerry sat me down and made me do what he called 'number-crunching'. The very thought of the phrase gives me shivers. He made me make a list of all my outgoings, future commitments and regular income. He did the same for himelf, and then we (or rather he) totted everything up. It didn't look good at first, and some things had to be crossed off the outgoings list. One major expense that I resolved to put a red line through was working in Bristol, which, amazingly, was costing me more than £400 a month in fuel and toll fees. Relocating to Cardiff sorted that little problem out.

As much as I hated staring at our monthly expenditure in black and white, I appreciated how important it was. It really is the only way to check whether you will be able to make ends meet or not, and it is an excellent way of examining your regular spending and seeing whether some things are that important to you.

The first step is to work out, as best you can, what you owe, what repayments you make, and any other regular 'essential' outgoings you have – food, travel, insurance, subscriptions, etc. Allow some additional costs for, say, clothes, entertainment, hobbies and interests. I'm not going to waste any time preaching about ways to save money – there are plenty of self-help books and internet sites which will help you do that. What I will pass on is one trick that helped for me. What I learned to do before making a purchase was to say to myself: 'Do I really need this, or do I just want it.' I soon found the 'want' column was far longer than the 'need' one.

Case Study

Carolyn Ekins set up *www.acountrylife.com*, a website for smallholders and downshifters which proved invaluable to myself and Gerry when we were just starting out. In 1999, she moved from London to Carmarthenshire with husband David and three school-age children. By 2004, the family was making a further move – to Nova Scotia in Canada.

We bought our first smallholding in Wales back in 1999. David was in a well-paid job so we took out a large mortgage of around £125,000 and used some capital to pay the deposit. We were left with around £12,000 in the bank and, even though David continued to work, by the end of the first year that money had gone. We didn't splash out on stuff that was not needed. Things needed doing that, in our inexperienced first-timers' way, we hadn't budgeted for. A big expense was the fencing – three whole fields needed doing. David was working long hours to pay the mortgage, so we had to get some friends of ours in to do it. The cost was very reasonable, but still a big chunk – around £2,000.

The other things soon added up. We needed an old tractor and a livestock trailer, and then there were animals to buy and feed, insurance, medication, vets bills, and an extra car, as I needed to bring the children to school. All these things were purchased as frugally as possible but they soon added up.

So that he wouldn't have to work away all week, David decided to take a job which allowed him to commute on a daily basis but, as this was in Wales rather than London, our income was dramatically reduced, and we began to eat into our capital.

I think we then realised that to have a large mortgage and successfully run a smallholding without having to work full-time was virtually impossible without something giving. Health begins to suffer and stress starts to build.

I think what we have learned over the years has been valuable. In a way, it's been good to make mistakes. At one stage we had twenty-five sheep and lambs, four pigs, two horses, six goats, two cows, ducks, geese and chickens. For one person on a day-to-day basis, that is too much of a workload. Also, it's expensive buying hay during the winter if you can't take an adequate hay cut off your own fields.

Carolyn and David Ekins set up a website for smallholders and downshifters after escaping the rat-race.

Now we are in Nova Scotia we will do things differently. Second time around, we will do things on a very small scale and actually will probably raise just a couple of lambs and weaners per year by buying them in rather than breeding them ourselves. I would hope, this time, to put more time and effort into growing our own food.

I think there is quite a big difference when you run a smallholding to make an income. Inevitably, costs spiral and more land and equipment is needed.

This time round we will be thinking small and self-sufficient.

4

CHOOSING YOUR SMALLHOLDING

ONE ESTATE agent I spoke to whilst researching this book said what a lot of people were looking for was a property with sufficient land to provide a kind of *'cordon sanitaire'* – a buffer zone between themselves and the outside world. Well, that's part of it. Those with high-pressure jobs who live stressful lives have always wanted their rural playgrounds with space for a couple of horses. However, a growing number of people in pursuit of the perfect smallholding are looking for a more fulfilling and totally different lifestyle – one which often involves growing their own produce and raising livestock for meat.

High-profile TV programmes, in which evangelical celebrity chefs preach about the importance of local produce and food traceability, the benefits of rearing farm animals naturally, and in humane conditions, have persuaded many that the only way to be sure of what they are eating is to grow and raise it themselves. The general housing market may be entering a quiet period, but demand for smallholdings and farms is higher than ever, and finding a good one at an affordable price is becoming increasingly difficult.

In January 2008, *Country Smallholding* magazine reported that west Wales and east Anglia were proving the the most popular areas for people hunting for a smallholding. Edward Oldrey, a director of specialist agent Rural Scene, said that west Wales – and in particular, Carmarthenshire – was one of the top choices since Devon and Cornwall had been priced out of the market for many people. According to the Royal Institution of Chartered Surveyors, more than 40 per cent of those buying farmland in Wales in 2007 were non-farmers – and among them were investors from other parts of the UK and overseas. Farmland prices were rising steadily, the survey said, with prices in Wales showing a 21 per cent increase on the previous year – a trend that looks set to continue.

The estate agent Savills reported in January 2008 that land in Wales cost an average of £2,903 an acre, and it predicted a further rise of 15 per cent in 2008 to £3,388. The price rise could lead to an increase in the amount of land being put up for sale. It's now common to see holdings in Wales – some with just a handful of acres of land – advertised in the local press for over £1m. Equally, it's still possible to buy a farmhouse with land for as little as £250,000 here – as long as you're not fussy about the location and don't mind renovation work.

If, like me, you're a 'know it when you see it' type of home-buyer, you have my sympathies. Finding your dream home is rarely an easy process. Getting through the minefield of red tape and legal pitfalls between making an offer and completing the sale can be even more difficult. And when you're looking for a smallholding, your problems are a hundred times worse. You no longer just thinking about four walls and maybe a garden. Now your all-important checklist will have to include a whole host of factors relating to the land surrounding the property.

It helps, of course, if you have a clear idea of what you are looking for. So just what do you WANT?

Location, Location, Location!

- Is the geographical location vitally important to you, or is your work or domestic situation sufficiently flexible to allow you to consider a wide radius of potential places?
- Would you prefer to be near major towns or cities, or have easy access to motorways, railway or bus stations?
- Do you want to be within walking distance of schools, shops, local amenities?
- Are you concerned about your home being in an isolated position (particularly if yourself or your partner is going to be away from home some of the time)? Or do you feel that the fewer houses near you the better?
- If the smallholding is in a remote place – maybe up an unmade track, for instance – would you have to invest in a 4 x 4 (or two)?
- Are views important to you? How would you feel about a pylon a few metres away from your front door? What if there was a rubbish dump or a scrapyard on neighbouring land?
- Do you want to be near a main road, so that you can sell produce at the farm gate?
- What do the neighbours do? Would their day-to-day operations cause you problems or conflict with your plans – or might they object to some of your plans? Is there a really busy time of day – and if so, why? Would you mind if the milk tanker blocked the road every day, bringing all traffic to a standstill for half an hour?
- What are current relations like with the neighbours, and are there any boundary disputes? The vendor has a legal duty to tell you.
- Would you have to share access with a neighbouring property and, if so, would you have to pay towards ongoing maintenance?

Buildings and Services

- Is there an agricultural tie on the holding which limits residency to someone whose primary income is derived from agricultural or horticultural activities? If so, could you meet the necessary criteria? Holdings with agricultural ties can cost up to 25 per cent less than those without, so it can look a tempting proposition. Equine activities – such as running a livery yard or riding stables – don't count, by the way. In some cases it is possible to have the restriction lifted or modified – and an increasing number of private companies offer to do the legwork and make the application on your behalf for a hefty fee – but don't be persuaded to buy on this basis, because there are no guarantees.
- Is there an existing house, or are you looking at buying a building plot or a derelict barn to convert? If there is a house, is it in an acceptable state of repair? If not, are you prepared for major renovation work and the time, inconvenience and costs involved?
- Does the property have mains electricity, water and sewerage? How would you feel about having water from a bore-hole or a spring? What if your household waste goes into a septic tank, or even a primitive soak-away? Could you unblock it yourself, in an emergency?
- Are there outbuildings for storage and livestock, or would you have to erect some? What kind of costs would be involved – and could you get planning permission? What if you buy and then find out you can't get consent?
- Are you thinking of running a business from your smallholding? Would you need 'change of use' planning permission? Is there sufficient space? Is the existing access suitable, or might you need to create a new access, which could require planning permission?
- Are any of the buildings considered to be of architectural importance – perhaps with listed status? If so, any repairs or modifications will have to be carried out with the approval of Cadw, the division of the Welsh Assembly which protects the historic environment of Wales. There may be an ancient monument on the land which requires you to give access to the general public. Cadw can provide advice and, in some cases, grants towards the upkeep of monuments and historic buildings. Visit *www.cadw.wales.gov.uk* or ring 01443 33 6000 for advice.

The Land

- What is the land like? Is it good-quality agricultural land, or would it require a lot of work to improve? Is the soil free-draining, or does it turn into a quagmire at the first sign of rain? Is there any likelihood of serious flooding (check with Environment Agency Wales).
- Is the soil stony? This may seem a minor inconvenience in the great scheme of

things, but have you ever spent several weeks digging holes for trees or gateposts in soil which is full to the gunnels with rocks and boulders?

▨ If you intend to grow crops to feed livestock, or perhaps a market garden venture, is the land suitable? Do you want organic status? Converting to organic takes at least two years, so bear this in mind. The Welsh Assembly Government provides financial support to farmers who wish to convert to organic farming through the Organic Farming Scheme for Wales. Ring the Organic Centre Wales helpline on 01970 622100 or visit the website *www.organic.aber.ac.uk*.

▨ What direction does the land face, how high is it and how much rain or sunshine does it get? How strong are the prevailing winds?

▨ Is there a reliable water supply to the fields, or could you install one? If you'll be keeping livestock, you won't want to be carrying buckets across your fields day and night. Similarly, growing crops could prove a nightmare without adequate irrigation.

▨ If the land had public rights of way crossing it, would you mind? How comfortable might you be about strangers walking over your land – maybe even through your garden? How would you feel about having to pay for the upkeep of footpaths and stiles, plus the possibility of extra fencing to separate ramblers and dog-walkers from your livestock?

▨ Is there adequate fencing and/or hedging to safely contain livestock? If not, how much work and expense would be involved to put it right?

▨ Is some or all of the land designated a Special Site of Scientific Interest (SSSI), or subject to some other designation imposed to protect habitat or special features? If so, there will be constraints upon its use.

▨ And finally … how much land do you think you will need, and for what purpose? If, for instance, you're thinking of keeping horses or livestock, you need to be looking for sufficient land to allow you to move your animals when the ground needs a rest. You may also want to grow your own fodder and bedding, which means adding even more acres to your shopping list.

Wet, Wet Wales: Some Things to Bear in Mind

Physical characteristics impose limits on everyone and everything. Wales is a nation which has heavier rainfall, more mountainous land and generally poorer soil quality than the majority of farming regions in England. It is no surprise, therefore, that agriculture in Wales has become far less reliant on crop-growing and more geared towards livestock production than most other parts of the UK. Much higher rainfall levels (almost double some parts of England) causes waterlogging and loss of nutrients, ruling out successful cultivation of a wide variety of crops. Welsh agriculture is dominated by livestock production, with dairy, beef and sheep accounting for 75 per cent of the value of gross output. Cereal crops are largely a thing of the past, with more and more farmers buying in bedding straw and winter feeds; hay-making has long given way to silage production, mainly because grass cut for silage does not need so much drying-out time.

Topography is a major factor – if not *the* major factor – in deciding how we use our land. In Wales, the total land area is around 2.1m ha, of which, 1.7m ha (81 per cent) is being used for some kind of agricultural purpose. Around 60 per cent of the land is more than 150m above sea level, while 27 per cent is more than 300m above sea level. This high altitude, when combined with sheer inclines and heavy rainfall, means poor soils.

The majority (around 80 per cent) of agricultural land in Wales is classified as low-grade; this is reflected in the proportion of land designated as being in Less Favoured Areas (LFA). The designation is given because of the presence of infertile land with limited potential, which produces economic returns appreciably lower than the UK average. These areas also possess low and dwindling populations largely dependent on agriculture. There is a total of 1.6m ha of LFA land in Wales, of which, 1.1m ha (69 per cent) is used for agricultural purposes. By comparison, 57 per cent of England's LFA land is used for agriculture.

The combination of factors affecting farmland in Wales has led to a higher proportion of the land being turned over to grassland production than in some areas. More than 83 per cent of our agricultural land is permanent grassland or used for rough grazing. By comparison, just 5 per cent is used for tillage crops. The best land – Grade 1 and Grade 2 – is found in the north-east, around Flint and Wrexham, in parts of the Vale of

Isolation is one factor affecting the choice of location.

Glamorgan, and small pockets in south Pembrokeshire and south Gower. These are the areas where physical characteristics pose little limitation to agriculture. The land is relatively level, rainfall is lower than elsewhere in Wales and the soils are deep, fertile and well-drained.

The $64,000 Question: How Much Land?

The average person has no idea how big an acre is. Gerry and I certainly didn't before we moved, and I still have trouble if put on the spot and asked to come up with a good 'guesstimate' of how big a particular field might be. In any case, as the saying goes, it's not what you've got but how you use it.

Five acres of good-quality, flattish, free-draining land, free of obstacles can often be worth more than 25 acres which is dominated by steep, rocky ground that can't be cultivated or dense woodland. Be wary, therefore, of estate agents' brochures which quote acreage: there may, indeed, be 50 acres of land with the property you're looking at, but huge swathes might well be unusable for anything other than grazing sheep.

Pony paddocks – little scraps of land here and there without buildings or planning permission – are being snapped up for silly prices by affluent, town-dwelling horselovers. And competition can force prices are going through the roof when land is sold at auction. Just look at this article, published in the *Western Mail* in April 2006:

Auction bidders duel over paddock

Local farmers and pony owners stood spellbound last week as McCartneys auctioneers knocked down a paddock on the edge of Talgarth for £22,200 an acre.

The 4.8-acre field is alongside one of the radial routes out of Talgarth, well outside the development limits. But the level of interest shown beforehand and the shortage of small areas of land on the market had given a clear indication that the demand was going to be fairly hot. Two determined bidders refused to let go, going from an opening bid of £25,000 until the bidding ended at £107,000 – more than £22,000 an acre.

McCartneys partner and auctioneer Ryan Williams said valuing small areas of land was one of the hardest tasks the company had to carry out. 'There is a common misconception amongst the general public that all farmland is worth £2,000 to £4,000 an acre,' he said. 'The reality is that the current demand for land is intense and the smaller the acreage the more per acre that land will make.'

Local demand will have a bearing on how much land you can afford in any given area, but let's get back to the big question: how much land do you really need? If all you want is a comfort zone of greenery between you and the rest of the world, somewhere for your dog to run around safely, and sufficient space for a few chickens to scratch about, you might be happy with a house surrounded by as little as an acre. But if you

Table I. Ideas of what might be achieved on holdings of varying sizes

Size of holding	Sufficient space for
Example 1 *Large garden,* *0.5 to 1 acre*	▓ an extensive fruit and vegetable plot – maybe even a few fruit trees – plus a greenhouse or small polytunnel, which could supply produce all year round ▓ a dozen or so chickens for eggs and/or meat; maybe a small pond and duck house (again, eggs and/or meat), and even a rabbit run, if you've a penchant for rabbit pie or bunny burgers ▓ beehives – for the production of honey and other products, and also to encourage pollination of fruit and vegetable crops and trees ▓ small workshop/food preparation area/shop for produce
Example 2 *5 acres*	All of the above, plus ▓ fodder crops for livestock (see below), along with EITHER ▓ a few weaners to be reared for pork or bacon and to provide manure for the veg patch ▓ some goats to produce milk (for you and the pigs) and/or meat for the table, plus some more useful manure OR ▓ a small breeding flock of sheep (no more than a dozen) OR ▓ stabling and limited grazing for a few horses, llamas or alpacas OR ▓ hiring out fields to neighbouring farmers
Example 3 *10 acres*	All listed in *Example 1*, plus your choice from *Example 2*, and ▓ a cow or two and calves (producing milk for yourselves and the pigs – if you have them – plus meat and fertilizer)

Note: Each example is assumed to be a lowland holding in an area with average rainfall and with workable soil.

have more ambitious plans, you have to think more carefully. It's a bit like the 'how long is a piece of string?' conundrum; there are a myriad of potential answers, and no two people are going to agree. Factors range from geography and climate to your chosen style of farming, attitude to animal welfare and the amount of cash you have at your disposal.

Your first step has to be deciding how you want to live, how much food you want to be able to produce and whether or not you want to try and go the whole hog and be totally self-sufficient. As a general rule of thumb, the better the location, climate and soil quality, the less land you will need. Similarly, owners of smaller sized holdings often find they manage their land in a much more careful and economical way, in an effort to achieve maximum results. Again, it all depends on your style of land and livestock management. Personally, I prefer to rotate the use of fields regularly – for common sense reasons I'll explain later. I also like to have space available to allow stock to be moved at short notice if necessary; others more dependent on producing as much as possible out of their land will opt for a more intensive approach.

I must stress that the table only gives examples of what can be accommodated – we all have our own personal preferences, and our own ideas of how space can be used. The key thing to remember is *don't underestimate* how much land you will need – particularly for grazing. Newcomers to livestock-keeping are often surprised at how quickly their animals devour or trample vegetation, and get round the problem by buying in fodder to supplement what they have available. But food supply is not the only factor here: to ensure healthy livestock, you have to be able to move them to fresh ground on a regular basis.

As well as over-grazing and poaching of the ground in wet weather, you have to be aware that too many animals continually grazing one area of land will increase parasitic worm burden in the soil, too. Under-grazing, on the other hand, can be detrimental to grassland, and to the conservation value of your land; grassland will quickly revert to scrub if not grazed or cut mechanically at the appropriate times, so it really is worth talking to experienced farmers or professional agricultural advisers for advice on planning an effective grassland management regime. See also Chapter 9.

Starting off your Search

We're all busy people, and no one likes wasting time – particularly when it comes to house-hunting. Whether you're moving to Wales for the first time, or planning to re-locate from one part of Wales to another, you'll need to do your research. Leaving it all to the estate agents is likely to get you nowhere. Unless you're the kind of person that closes their eyes and sticks a pin in a map, you will probably have a rough idea of which part of Wales you want to move to, the type of property you want, and you'll have a list of priorities and preferences about a whole range of other features, as we discussed in the previous chapter.

Local newspapers
Despite the influence of the internet on the property market, local papers are still the first-stop shop, in my opinion. Whereas property websites will give you great access to a whole range of holdings for sale, local papers will, in addition, have all those other ads from private sellers keen for a quick sale. Once you have narrowed down your search to a few key areas of Wales, find out the names of the local weeklies and get them sent to you each week. It is only going to cost about 50p a week for each paper. The big plus

point is that, as well as access to the property pages, you'll also be getting the news from the community you're considering joining. You might even pick up some early warnings about potential developments – good or bad – which may help you to refine your search even further.

There are two daily papers in Wales. One is the *Western Mail* (tel. 029 20223333; *www.walesonline.co.uk*), which has the bulk of its readership concentrated in south and west Wales, gradually declining as you venture past mid-Wales and up into the north. In north Wales, the *Daily Post* (tel. 01492 574455; *www.icnorthwales.co.uk*) reigns supreme. Both papers have substantial property supplements on Saturdays, often featuring private ads for smallholdings and parcels of land. It is definitely worth placing an order for whichever one is best for your search.

Dealing with Estate Agents

Embarking on the search for your property should be a bit easier by now, so the next thing is to enlist a little professional help. Finding a good estate agent is easier said than done, and it pays to make sure you get in touch with the right ones. The average high street estate agent deals mainly with average homes, and only occasionally gets a smallholding on the books, so seek out the specialists in rural properties. Again, go back to the local papers, and check out which agencies appear to be the most appropriate. I've added a list of some estate agents which deal regularly in smallholdings and farms at the end of this chapter. It's not an exhaustive list, and I'm sure you'll find more. If you do find some good ones, let me know and I may include them when I update this book.

Just as finding the best estate agents can be a trial, ensuring that the agency sends you details of appropriate properties can be difficult. What you don't want is a whole load of details of totally unsuitable places dropping through your letterbox every day, so make sure the agency knows *exactly* what you want. If you say you want a three-bedroom property with 'a bit of land', expect to be sent everything ranging from houses with large gardens to intensive grassland farms covering several hundred acres. Be as specific as you can and you'll make your job – and theirs – a lot easier.

I thought I'd try an experiment to see just how useful and efficient estate agents could be and was rather disillusioned. I e-mailed a handful of them, telling them the sort of property I wanted. I gave them the locations I was interested in, a minimum acreage (20+), and a realistic maximum guide price (£600,000). What I got in return was both surprising and disappointing: a flurry of useless particulars on detached houses with nothing more than large gardens, and a handful of holdings with between two and five acres.

It wasn't even as if there weren't any properties available which met the specified criteria – a quick look at their websites confirmed there were a number of places which matched the acreage and the price range perfectly. For some unknown reason, whoever was in charge of stuffing envelopes just hadn't paid sufficient attention to the brief, and seemed to have sent anything containing the word 'smallholding'.

My wholly unscientific survey convinced me that it's not good enough just to e-mail your details off and hope for the best. The only way of getting what you want, rather than what someone thinks you *might* want is to deal direct with the estate agent, make contact on a regular basis and build up a rapport.

Whittling Down the Properties

So the weekend is coming and you've been sent a good wodge of properties to visit. Time is short, so which ones are you going to see? You might know the rough areas where the properties are located from previous visits, maybe holidays, but you need to decide which holdings you should spend your precious time on, before jumping into the car and driving what might be hundreds of miles.

Your first step should be to ring the estate agent. Grill the sales person about the location, proximity of shops and other amenities, and find out as much as possible to help build up a mental picture of what it would be like driving up to the site. Staff will live locally, so will probably know the place like the back of their hands, or will be able to pass you on to someone who does. Ring the local post office, too – if it hasn't been shut down and turned into a shop selling knitted baby clothes or eco-friendly kaftans and bits of driftwood shaped into fruit bowls. People in Wales love to talk more than anything else in the world, and can't resist an invitation to talk about our their communities.

How are your map-reading skills? If you haven't looked at an Ordnance Survey map for years, it's time to rediscover this gem of a resource. Either buy one for the area which covers your search zone – the Explorer maps are best – or go to the internet and search using a website like *www.multimap.com*. If you remember your geography lessons (or if you can borrow a child studying the subject at school), you should be able to get a fair idea of the area you're thinking of visiting.

Google Earth (*earth.google.com* – note, no need to use the 'www' prefix) is an absolutely excellent – if slightly addictive – resource, providing satellite pictures of actual locations and even 3D images of buildings. Typing in an address allows you to fly to a property and zoom right in for a look. It may not work on some older computers, and it is best accessed with a broadband connection rather than dial-up, so check out the required specifications first.

Viewing a Property

Your viewing day has arrived, so it's all systems go. It's so easy to get caught up in all the excitement of the great adventure that there's a danger you'll forget a lot of things you really need to check out and ask about. Go back to the beginning of this chapter and make yourself your own checklist of what you want and don't want from a smallholding. Don't be afraid to ask awkward questions, because you're the one who's going to have to live in the place, and if you don't find out now, you could end up making a costly and unpleasant mistake.

As decent smallholdings in Wales are becoming more and more scarce, don't be surprised if you end up viewing the place with a number of other potential buyers. Our viewing day was like being on a school trip around Blenheim Palace, with three other couples squeezing into the rooms and dodging the low beams along with us as the estate agent acted as tour guide, pointing out the blatantly obvious. Group viewings aren't the best way of seeing a house, because you don't feel free to point out interesting or attractive features to your partner, for fear someone else might spot them, too. We arranged a second visit – without all the other house-hunters – and made an offer on the spot.

Depending on the list of priorities you have drawn up, you will have a good idea of which aspects of the holding you want to explore at length. Don't forget to take the list with you, and don't be embarrassed to make notes as you go along. Take a camera with you, too – maybe even a video camera – because you'll be surprised how fuzzy the memory gets by the time you're back home.

When you've completed your viewing and are satisfied you have no more questions to ask, go to the pub! Yes, you've deserved a nice pub lunch after all that hard work, but your main reason for visiting the local is to do a little bit more fact-finding. It may help you find out more about the property you've been to see, and the area you're thinking of joining.

To Buy or Not to Buy?

You might find there is a great deal of interest in the property, and this can have a big influence on your eagerness to put in an offer. If so, sit down, dig out that checklist (you know, the one you dropped in the slurry when the geese chased you) and systematically go through every one of the points you noted down prior to your visit.

One final word of advice at this stage: get yourself a good solicitor. You're not buying a 'normal' property, so you need someone with experience of carrying out searches on farmland. Grill potential candidates to make sure they are up to the job.

ESTATE AGENTS TO TRY
Bob Jones-Prytherch and Co. (*www.bjpco.com*), tel. 01267 236363. Offices in Carmarthen, Haverfordwest, Llandeilo, Narberth and St Clears
The Smallholding Centre (*www.thesmallholdingcentre.co.uk*), tel. 01239 851242. Based in Newcastle Emlyn in Ceredigion. Specializes in the sale of smallholdings and rural properties throughout Ceredigion, Carmarthenshire and Pembrokeshire.
Clee Tompkinson Francis (*www.ctf-uk.com*), tel. 01267 230645. Sells properties throughout Wales and the Border Counties and has 11 offices in 6 counties.

Evans Bros (*www.evansbros.co.uk*), tel. 01267 236611. Offices in Carmarthen, Llanybydder, Lampeter, and Aberaeron. Properties for sale across west and mid-Wales.

Roderick Price (*www.roderickprice.co.uk*), tel. 0267 230571. Sells properties across south and west Wales.

Terry Thomas (*www.terrythomas.co.uk*), tel. 01267 235865 or 235330. Carmarthenshire, Pembrokeshire and Ceredigion.

John Francis (*www.johnfrancis.co.uk*), tel. 1267 233111. Has 18 offices covering south and west Wales.

Rural Scene (*www.ruralscene.co.uk*), tel. 01264 850700. Website promoting properties across Wales.

Smallholding Wales (*www.smallholding-wales.co.uk*). Website promoting properties in west and mid-Wales.

West Wales Properties (*www.westwalesproperties.co.uk*), tel. 01437 762893. Offices across west Wales.

Prime Location (*www.primelocation.com*). Website promoting properties across Wales.

Profile Homes (*www.profilehomes.com*), tel. 01550 777790. Country and equestrian property specialists, based in Carmarthenshire, selling properties in mid-, west and north Wales.

Property Place Wales (*www.propertyplacewales.com*), tel. 01267 221222. Based in Carmarthen and specializing in properties in and around Carmarthenshire.

Herbert R. Thomas (*www.hrt.uk.com*), tel. 01446 772911. Offices in Cowbridge and Neath.

Bob Parry Estate Agents (*www.bobparry.co.uk*), tel. 01286 673 286. Offices in Blaenau Ffestiniog, Caernarfon, Harlech, Llangefni, Llanrwst, Porthmadog and Pwllheli.

Welsh Property (*www.welshproperty.co.uk*), tel. 08456 449342. Based in Ammanford, Carmarthenshire, selling properties in west and mid-Wales.

Bowen Son & Watson (*www.bowensonandwatson.co.uk*), tel. 01978 340000. Offices in Chirk and Wrexham.

Dafydd Hardy (*www.dafyddhardy.co.uk*), tel. 01248 371212. Offices in Bangor, Caernarfon and Llandudno.

Warriner's (*www.warriners.co.uk*), tel. 01248 354002. Properties in Snowdonia, Gwynedd and Anglesey.

Sheridan Jones Estate Agents (*www.sheridanjonesestateagents.co.uk*), tel. 01248 717176. Based in the town of Menai Bridge, Anglesey.

Burnells Estate Agents (*www.northwales-property.co.uk*), tel. 01407 762165. Based in Holyhead, Anglesey.

Robbie Howarth Estate Agent (*www.robbie-howarth.co.uk*), tel. 01492 572213. Selling properties in Llandudno, Conwy, Deganwy, Glan Conwy, Penrhyn Bay, Rhos on Sea, Colwyn Bay, Llandudno Junction, the Conwy Valley and surrounding areas.

Reeds Rains (*www.reedsrains.co.uk*), tel. 01745 832150. Sells properties across north Wales, with offices in Abergele, Conwy and in Cheshire.

Walter Lloyd Jones & Co (*www.w-lloydjones.com*), tel. 01341 422278. Offices in Barmouth and Dolgellau.

St David's Estate Agents (*www.stdavidsproperty.co.uk*), tel. 01492 534881. Offices in Colwyn Bay and Rhyl and covering the whole of the north Wales coast and the Conwy Valley.

Huw Tudor & Sons (*www.huwtudor.co.uk*), tel. 01758 701100. Based in Pwllheli.

Joan Hopkin Estate Agents (*www.joan-hopkin.co.uk*), tel. 01248 810847. Based in Beaumaris, Anglesey.

J. Merfyn Pugh (*www.jmerfynpugh.co.uk*), tel. 01758 701888 Based in Pwllheli, Gwynedd.

David Parry & Co (*www.davidparry.co.uk*), tel. 0844 567 0007. Sells properties throughout Wales and the Border Counties.

5

GETTING READY TO MOVE

P REPARATION IS EVERYTHING if you want to make your move as stress-free as possible. The time between having your offer accepted and actually getting the keys in your hand can seem an absolute age when you're really keen to get in and start living your exciting new lifestyle, but this achingly long period should be put to good use. I'll start talking about the practical, nuts-and-bolts side of getting ready for your move, and then go on to discuss some of the smallholding-related things you might want to consider researching while you're waiting for the arrival of your big day and the start of your great adventure.

The first thing you should be doing is making a list of things you need to do as moving day approaches. As with any house move, there will be a whole host of things you may need to do, from sorting out paperwork with utility companies, mortgage and insurance brokers, to arranging children's school places and transport.

How far ahead you start your count-down will depend on your own circumstances, but three months before the expected completion date will give you plenty of time to sort most things. Even before you agree on a moving-in date, you can start doing one essential job – having a good old sort out and getting rid of all that junk and clutter. Believe me, when you take on a smallholding, you'll start to accumulate even more, so you don't want to be taking your old stuff with you as well. Get the best bits listed on eBay, take other items to a car boot sale, and share the remainder between your local charity shops.

Other Things to Consider

▪ Book a removal company or hire yourself a self-drive van in plenty of time. Word-of-mouth recommendations are best, but try and find a firm which belongs to the British Association of Removers (BAR) or the National Guild of Removers and Storers (NGRS).

- Start wrapping up valuables and anything you know you won't be using in the coming weeks and source a supply of strong boxes. List the contents on the outside of the box to help easy sorting.
- Make some change-of-address cards.
- Find out who supplies your electricity, gas or oil, etc., and shop around for the best deals.

A month before moving

- You should have a completion date by now, so start contacting everyone with your new address.
- Arrange to get your mail redirected for at least the first three months after moving in.
- Start packing in earnest. Things like summer or winter clothes which won't be needed (depending on the season you're moving) can be packed away, along with Christmas decorations and so on. Don't forget to label the boxes!
- Think about the contents of your freezer and food cupboards, and start eating your way through; don't buy more than you need.

A week or two before moving

- Call in favours from family and friends to help you on moving day. Those who aren't able to help with moving heavy furniture and boxes may agree to take on child or pet-sitting duties, or prepare you some meals to heat up at the end of your first day.
- Defrost your fridge and freezer.
- Cancel milk and newspaper deliveries and settle bills.
- Send out final moving notification letters.
- Double-check with your estate agent and solicitor that everything is going to plan regarding the transfer of funds and handover of keys; confirm arrangements with the removal for van hire firm.
- Arrange insurance cover for your new property – and don't forget any outbuildings.

The day before moving

Pack a box of essential items: tea and coffee-making items, kettle, toilet rolls, light bulbs, bed linen – plus wine and corkscrew for later in the day, of course. Keep these with you rather than putting them in the removal van. Also keep any valuables or important documents with you.

Moving-in day!

Thanks to a series of delays, administrative problems, poor communication and misunderstandings, our 'moving-in day' stretched into an entire weekend. I'll spare you the horrid, frustrating details. Gerry and I had both taken time off work – him from his high-powered and demanding role with the police and me from a media job I had started just a few weeks before – and we were working to a pretty tight schedule. Sometimes I think moving house would be so much easier if it were just the vendor and the buyer involved. Moving home, as everyone knows, is one of the most stressful experiences of life, but take comfort from this: however bad you think yours is, ours was a hundred times worse. It was enough to put us off moving again – at least for a few years.

Apart from making sure that both your solicitor and the vendor's solicitor know what they are doing, the best advice for moving-in day is to plan well in advance. As I mentioned earlier, get as much packed as is humanly possible and try and get children and pets farmed out to friends or relatives. Then at least you and your partner will only have one another – and, of course, the people helping you to transport your stuff – to shout at if things go wrong.

The other golden rule is to make sure all your boxes are labelled – particularly the ones containing tea and coffee-making items, packed lunch, bottles of wine, and the corkscrew. Numerous tea breaks are essential to any successful house move, and I believe a good few glasses of something seriously alcoholic are almost compulsory at the end of a day when you feel thoroughly exhausted and fit for no more.

Preparation – for Yourself and your Smallholding

Moving to a smallholding can be far more complex than simply moving house and, as you'll see when you come to the livestock section of this book, I'm a great believer in forward-planning and doing homework before going too far. I'm assuming that, if you've been contemplating such a move for some time, you'll have found yourself a few good books about running a smallholding, growing your own produce, and rearing whatever animals you're considering. If you haven't, take a look at the recommended reading list at the end of this chapter and, for books and websites about specific animals, see the relevant sections in Chapter 8.

There are some really useful monthly magazines which are worth seeking out. My personal favourite is *Country Smallholding* (www.countrysmallholding.com), which is a really nicely produced publication. It has a good mail order section, through which you can buy books and videos, and lots of classified ads from breeders and livestock supplies companies. Its rival, *Smallholder* (www.smallholder.co.uk), is just as good for content, but less well-written, less slickly produced and therefore I find it less appealing to read. Like the previous magazine mentioned, it has lots of small ads for livestock and equipment.

Drawing up plans for your land
One thing you can be doing while you're counting the days until you become a landowner is to create a rough blueprint of what you would like to do with your

holding. You might, for instance, need to stock-fence your boundaries or get hedges planted or laid, and it's worth, in this limbo time, to assess the likely costs involved. You will probably have a sketch map of the holding from the estate agent which will give field sizes, but if not, ask the vendor or arrange to have the land measured. Only then will you be able to get an idea of what materials are likely to cost, and you'll be able to ring around local contractors for quotes.

Similarly, you might want to work out the cost of erecting outbuildings or getting existing ones into a usable condition. Use the time to get in touch with the planning department of the local council to see whether permission will be needed. Do the leg-work now and you'll save yourself a lot of frustration further down the line. If you're planning to buy livestock, work out what accommodation and equipment you will need, where it's going to come from, how long it will take and what it's going to cost. The same goes for the animals: once you've decided what you want, locate relevant breeders and see when they are likely to have stock to sell; good stock can't just be bought 'off the peg'.

Join a farming union

You may find it useful to join one of the farming unions. The National Farmers' Union and the Farmers' Union of Wales both have offices throughout Wales and can offer advice on all aspects of your holding, including applying to join agri-environment schemes and specialist insurance cover:

NFU Cymru, Agriculture House, Royal Welsh Showground, Builth Wells, Powys LD2 3TU, tel. 01982 554200, fax 01982 554201 (*www.nfu-cymru.org.uk*).

Farmers' Union of Wales, Llys Amaeth, Plas Gogerddan, Aberystwyth SY23 3BT, tel. 01970 820820, fax 01970 820821 (*www.fuw.org.uk*).

Explore funding opportunities

Use some of your time to investigate any financial help – from the government and other sources – that may be on offer. Don't hold out too much hope, though. See Chapter 6 for more on this.

Get yourself trained up

There is no substitute for experience, so get yourself some training. Check the location of the nearest agricultural college and find out what courses are on offer. Most offer everything from one- or two-day introductions to subjects, to longer, more formal training courses which result in recognized educational qualifications. If you can enrol on a course offering an introduction to smallholding, you'll be getting a head start. The one I did at Pencoed College, Bridgend, gave a comprehensive overview of livestock-keeping, land management, use of farm machinery, and explained the legal side of things, too.

LANTRA, the skills agency for the land-based and environmental sector, works with colleges throughout Wales to provide training for farming families and employees. Depending on your situation, you may qualify for a discount on certain courses. I got 50 per cent of my smallholders' course fees paid, just because I had a holding number, but students on subsequent courses weren't so fortunate, because of constraints on funding. The organization's website (*www.lantra.co.uk*) has a course-finding facility which allows you to do a postcode search to find training within easy reach (or ring them on 0845 707 8007).

Short courses in subjects like sheep husbandry, tractor driving or hedgelaying and drystone walling are always popular. If your local agricultural college isn't running courses in traditional country skills, and if LANTRA can't help, conservation organizations like the British Trust for Conservation Volunteers (*www.btcvcymru.org*, 029 2052 0990) here in Wales or the Wildlife Trusts (*www.wildlifetrustswales.org*, 029 20480070, or *www.wildlifetrusts.org*, 01636 677711) outside Wales, often offer training opportunities to volunteers and organize work parties so you can practise your newly learned techniques.

Increasingly, experienced livestock-keepers are realizing the gaps in the market for good-quality training at an affordable price. Be wary, though, as some husbandry courses for beginners may cost you more than you bargained for. The price of the course itself may sound good, but you may be tempted to buy stock and equipment from your affable hosts, only to find that you've paid way over the odds. It can seem easy to buy all you need from a 'one-stop-shop', but it pays to take your time and go for the best deal, so check prices elsewhere before committing yourself.

Two of my old college tutors, Phil Thomas and David John, set up their own business, Down to Earth Services (*www.downtoearthuk.net* or ring 01443 229203), as a way of supplementing income from their farms and have found there is a huge demand for short courses tailored to suit new landowners. They teach everything from animal husbandry to traditional country estate skills and also provide a bespoke consultancy service to help new smallholders, advising on things like different uses for land and applying for grants. In addition, they run courses for the more experienced livestock-keepers which include hands-on (or is that hands-in?) sessions on lambing and calving. I've attended some of Phil's lambing courses and they really gave me the confidence boost I needed when it came to lambing for the first time on my holding.

It can be difficult to find tutors with the experience and teaching ability of Phil and David, who are based in south Wales, but an internet trawl or a flick through the classified ads of specialist magazines may throw up a few. Tim and Dot Tyne run residential lambing courses at their farm in Pwllheli in north Wales (*www.viableselfsufficiency.co.uk* or ring 01758 721898), as well as providing a consultancy service.

Getting equipped
If you were to ask half a dozen different smallholders for a list of what they would consider 'essential equipment' for a new landowner, they would probably give you half a

dozen completely different replies. Until you know what you want to do with your land, what care it will need, and the geography and climate you're likely to be dealing with, it will all be pretty much a guessing game. I'm going to say something extremely sexist here, but men love buying tools and bits of machinery. Gerry's eyes light up when we visit a DIY store and so you can imagine his excitement when he realized our smallholding gave him the perfect excuse to stock up on what I call 'big boys' toys'.

Pretty soon, he had acquired a tractor mower, a chainsaw and a whole array of electrical gadgets, generators, air compressors, and a lot of items which defy description but I'm sure were really useful. Then came the bigger stuff: a 1967 McCormick International tractor and topper, a three-tonne mini-digger and the inevitable dumper truck.

You will be surprised at the machinery you will accumulate – and the skills you master.

It's a slippery slope which appears to have no end. In fairness to Gerry, though, he hasn't gone out and bought everything new. A lot of his most expensive purchases have come from eBay, classified ads in the local papers, farm dispersal sales and auctions – although I do occasionally wonder whether it might have made better economic sense to hire in a bit of kit for a particular job than invest good money in something that might only see some action once a year.

One alternative to forking out for equipment is to join a machinery ring. The Machinery Ring Association of England and Wales (*www.machineryrings.org.uk* or ring 01622 815356) is the umbrella body for ten different machinery rings. Open to all farmers, contractors, self-employed farm workers, mechanics, hire firms, etc. the ring has a database detailing the equipment and services its members offer. It works by matching up a member needing a particular piece of kit or service with someone who can supply it. Currently, there are rings covering north, mid, south and west Wales.

All of this raises an important question: when is it worth doing a job yourself, and when should you consider paying out to get someone else in? A good example of this is fencing. When Gerry and I first moved in, we did what we could to cut corners, and stock fencing was one of the jobs we thought we could do. Fencing, it turned out, wasn't our forte. We spent days and days trying to bang posts into incredibly stony ground, without any specialist equipment, and the end result was a wiggly fence and wobbly posts. A lot of time spent which could have been used doing freelance work to earn money to pay someone to do the job properly. Since then, we've always made it a rule not to skimp on jobs like fencing, which have to be done well. And we argue far less.

Bidding for bargains: the lure of the auction

Some people can't walk past a clothes shop or a car showroom. With me, it's farmers' marts. It's not just the atmosphere – although give me outdoor shopping in preference to neat and tidy chain stores filled with plasticky smells any day. The root of the obsession is undoubtedly the promise of a bargain, and the thrill of the chase in seeking it out. One of my favourites is the mart in Ffairfach, Llandeilo, held the last Saturday in every month. Don't confuse it with the kind of farmers' market that just sells local produce. Ffairfach has much more to offer than fruit and veg. Marts just like Ffairfach take place on a regular basis in all parts of rural Wales, so it won't be difficult to find one near you. Each will have its own character, quirks and peculiarities, and you'll have to do your homework to find out when you need to be there and how everything works.

At Ffairfach, there are usually four separate auctions taking place simultaneously – of poultry, new tools and DIY accessories, farm machinery, and, probably the most fascinating of all, a bizarre collection of bric-a-brac. As in most places, you have to register as a bidder (£1 in this case, paid in the little stone office next to none-too-fragrant men's toilets). Without a card bearing your buyer's number, you can't play – so don't forget!

The poultry auction is usually the first to kick off. It's the perfect opportunity if you're looking for your first flock, as you can browse the different breeds on offer and get advice from experienced breeders. For advice on buying livestock at auction, see

The great thing about auctions is that you never know what you will find.

Chapter 8. If you can brave the pushing and shoving, and the cacophony of clucking and quacking, amplified under the corrugated tin roof, you could go home with a bargain box of birds, or half a dozen eggs to try hatching out at home.

Similarly, if you're looking for a tractor, topper, trailer or a quad bike, you might strike lucky in the 'big boys' toys' section. Every auction brings an assortment, from farm vehicles to everyday cars, and finding what you want is really down to luck. We saw a decent-looking caravan go for just £80. Okay, it had orange and brown curtains and the interior was more 1970s than Marc Bolan, but it was worth saving – and even if you didn't want to reupholster, it would have done as a chicken house.

And so to the bric-a-brac. No rules here. It seems that everyone turns out the contents of their shed, barn or cupboard under the stairs, and plonks the contents in a box. But look beyond the old bathroom suites, broken lamps, and you may find curios like vintage milk churns, ploughs, mangles and seed drills which could make interesting garden ornaments, or which could be resold to others. You can tell there are bargains to be had by the number of dealers with non-local accents speaking surreptitiously into mobile phones and elbowing the locals out of the way.

The excitement of the auction is infectious, but the temptation to bid as soon as the auctioneer introduces the item you fancy should be avoided. He may start at £20, but if no one bites, he'll probably drop down to as low as a few pounds before the real bidding starts. Of course, by this point, you'll not be able to see what you're bidding for – auction-goers insist on packing themselves tightly around the auctioneer, and following him from lot to lot. The secret? Arrive a good hour before the sell-off is due to start, so you can have a good walk round and note down the lot numbers. Happy hunting!

Settling into your New Neighbourhood

Don't be surprised if you get neighbours turning up while you're trying to winch a wardrobe through a window or climb the stairs whilst balancing three boxes one on top of one another like a circus performer. The thing is, when you move into a small rural community, whether you like it or not, you're big news. The locals may leave it until after you've moved your furniture in before knocking on the door to introduce themselves, but you can guarantee that they will have heard all about you down at the local pub or in the village shop. Eventually, people will want to start doing their own research on you, so be prepared for the inquisition, and try not to be offended when they ask probing questions about your family, your background and your previous town or village. Think of it like a dog having a good old sniff to familiarize himself with the new arrival.

You might be brave enough to take the plunge completely and invite everyone round to meet you in your new home. Neighbours can rarely resist a housewarming, and it's a good way of killing lots of birds with one stone. It's also a good arena in which to drop hints about plans you have for the future which might affect neighbours or attract criticism or opposition, for example, building an extension, erecting a barn, or creating a new access to your property. It's much better to air these plans in a convivial setting rather than to let folk find out about things from a planning notice pinned to a lamp post.

Getting Involved

Becoming part of the community is vital if you want to be accepted, liked and respected. This is probably easier if you have young children, as school activities tend to suck in the help of parents like a sponge, and in a small, rural community the expectancy is going to be all the greater. Village organizations are always keen for new members and fresh blood, but don't be too pushy or you might end up stepping on someone's toes. Make it known that you are willing to help out, and, in the early days, at least, wait for people to make suggestions to you.

There are plenty of national organizations with active local branches, such as the Young Farmers' Clubs, the Women's Institute, Merched y Wawr (similar to the WI) and the Rotary Club. Your own personal interests and hobbies will undoubtedly create opportunities to meet new people, too. Lastly, if you're moving into a Welsh-speaking community, don't forget the advice I gave in Chapter 2. Make the effort to learn the language and see the difference it makes.

RECOMMENDED READING

Alan and Gill Bridgewater, *The Self-Sufficiency Handbook*, New Holland, 2007
Daniel Butler and Bel Crewe, *Urban Dreams, Rural Realities*, Pocket Books, 1999
Polly Ghazi and Judy Jones, *Downshifting: The Bestselling Guide to Happier, Simpler Living*,
    Hodder & Stoughton, 2004
Chas Griffin, *Scenes from a Smallholding*, Ebury, 2005
—— *More Scenes from a Smallholding*, Ebury, 2006
Jill Mason, *The Townies' Guide to the Countryside*, Merlin Unwin, 2003
John Seymour, *The New Complete Book of Self-Sufficiency*, Dorling Kindersley, 2003
Robin Shelton, *Allotted Time: Two Blokes, One Shed, No Idea*, Pan, 2007
Dick Strawbridge, *It's Not Easy Being Green*, BBC Books, 2006
Angela Sydenham, Bruce Monnington and Andrew Pym, *Essential Law for Landowners and
    Farmers*, Blackwell, 2002
Katie Thear, *The Smallholder's Manual*, Crowood Press, 2002
Paul Waddington, *21st Century Smallholder*, Eden Project Books, 2006

6

WHERE THERE'S MUCK...?

STORIES ABOUT farmers getting rich from agricultural subsidies carry about as much weight as stories of Welsh people talking English in a pub switching to the language of Heaven on the arrival of a tourist. The days when owners of vast areas of land in the best crop-growing regions of England supposedly lined their pockets by producing phenomenal amounts of cereals are long gone. Reform of the Common Agricultural Policy (CAP) around the turn of the twenty-first century brought about an end to the oft-criticized link between farm subsidies and production.

When the CAP was created in 1962, the idea was to guarantee regular food supplies at affordable prices and to ensure a fair standard of living for farmers. But, as environmental awareness grew through the decades, it was decided that, whilst there was still a need to produce high-quality food and to protect the rural economy, it should not be at the expense of the environment, the health and welfare of the animals, nor the future of the agricultural industry as a whole. The Single Payment Scheme (SPS), introduced in January 2005, and administered here by the National Assembly for Wales, replaced a whole raft of CAP subsidies which, effectively, had rewarded farmers for keeping large numbers of livestock and producing food in large quantities. The introduction of the SPS removed the incentive to produce more in order to secure subsidies – a process known as 'decoupling'. Instead of being paid in accordance with production, for the first time, farmers were given an annual payment based on the hectarage and value of the whole farm.

In order to receive payment, landowners must satisfy a list of criteria including having at least 0.3 ha (0.7 acre) of land at their disposal for at least ten continuous months of the year; be actively farming and/or maintaining the land in good agricultural and environmental condition; and maintaining up-to-date farm records (e.g. animal movements, veterinary treatments, etc.). At the heart of the SPS is the idea that landowners must farm in an environmentally friendly way, paying particular attention to controlling pollution, disposing of waste products efficiently and being careful about the use of

Farmers are no longer paid subsidies per animal. Instead, they are rewarded for environmentally friendly farming.

pesticides and fertilizers. Every year, a number of farms are chosen for inspection under the 'cross-compliance' regulations and, if a farm is shown not to be complying with any aspect of the rules, the SPS can be reduced or withheld. Landowners wishing to apply for the SPS must submit a Single Application Form to the National Assembly each May. There is a section on the form where farmers can apply to join agri-environment schemes.

What's on Offer?

More and more farmers are reaping the benefits of managing their land in a way that benefits nature – but don't get too excited, because there's a pretty big queue for places on the most successful agri-environment scheme. Tir Gofal (literally 'land in care' or 'care of the land') provides additional payments to farmers prepared to carry out work to enhance and protect wildlife and habitats, historical and landscape feature, and for improving public access to their land. Holdings must be a minimum of 3ha (approximately 7.4 acres), thus ruling out a great many smallholdings. Introduced by the

National Assembly in 1999, the scheme has proved proved immensely popular, so that the financial coffers are now looking pretty empty and no further funds appear to be forthcoming.

In March 2007, the Assembly took what was seen by many environmentalists as a retrograde step by voting to slash the budget for agri-environmental schemes in Wales, including Tir Gofal, by £2m per year. This was in order to boost the budget of another scheme, Tir Mynydd – the scheme designed to help hill farmers – which has social rather than environmental objectives.

At the time of writing (spring 2008), no more applications were being invited and, perhaps unsurprisingly, little up-to-date information was available on the Assembly website. I rang the Department for Rural Affairs and was told there was 'very little chance' of being able to join Tir Gofal. Only 500 applicants were being accepted each year, said the spokesman, and there was a considerable backlog already. Applying now would mean it would be likely to take up to three years to get accepted – but by then the scheme could have ended and another taken its place.

The Assembly is currently working on a review of all agri-environment schemes, which is likely to take effect from 2009. It is unlikely that agri-environment schemes will disappear altogether – particularly as the Welsh Assembly Government has made a commitment to halt the decline in biodiversity by 2010 – but there are doubts amongst conservationists that any successor scheme would be as beneficial to the countryside as Tir Gofal has been.

Since Tir Gofal was introduced it has paid around £100m to landowners and now covers 20 per cent of agricultural land in Wales. A report into the future of Tir Gofal from the Auditor General for Wales, published in November 2007, said the scheme had achieved its aims of helping to protect and enhance habitats, historic features and the natural beauty of the Welsh countryside, as well as increasing opportunities for public access to rural areas. It had also boosted the rural economy by £4.2m and created jobs. However, whilst the scheme was generally well-designed and managed, it cost more to run than was originally expected. The report said there were promising signs that Tir Gofal was improving the rural environment and had wider benefits, but without a long-term financial commitment the benefits achieved might not be sustainable.

So, if Tir Gofal is over-subscribed, what other alternatives are there? Well, basically, there is the much less popular entry-level scheme, Tir Cynnal ('maintenance of the land'). This scheme – described by my helpful man at the Assembly as 'the little sister of Tir Gofal' – puts fewer demands on the farmer. There are no stocking rate limits, but farmers still have to comply with requirements to prevent over-grazing. Whereas the driving force behind Tir Gofal is the creation of new habitats, landscape features and amenities, Tir Cynnal is more about preserving what exists. Biodiversity – the variety of wildlife on the farm – must not be lost, for instance, and every participating farm must have a minimum of 5 per cent of its area in a wildlife habitat such as broadleaved woodland, wetland, scrub, heathland, and unimproved grassland.

'Tir Cynnal is more about protecting what is already there,' explained my Assembly man.

It is pretty much a list of 'DON'Ts', whereas Tir Gofal is a list of 'DOs'. Tir Gofal encourages farmers to proactively look after the land. Tir Cynnal, on the other hand, was designed and developed to be a good first step for farmers. It was feared that, for a lot of people, the jump from being an average farmer to being a Tir Gofal farmer was too great.

Local Authority Grants

Biodiversity is the big buzz word in conservation circles and restoring biodiversity is one of the biggest challenges facing environmentalists. Many local authorities now offer biodiversity grants to landowners and community groups, so check with your council's biodiversity officer to see what's available. Details of how to contact your particular officer can be found on the Wales Biodiversity Partnership website *www.biodiversity-wales.org.uk* under the section 'Local to You'. The site also has information on grants available for individuals and groups under the section 'Get Involved'.

Monmouthshire County Council is just one example of a local authority being proactive in encouraging individuals to improve the environment. The council has been offering grants of up to £1,000 to help projects which benefit the local environment. These grants were offered through the Local Agenda 21 grant scheme and part-funded by the Countryside Council for Wales.

The council's Environment and Countryside Grant Scheme was designed to help people deliver projects of benefit to people and wildlife. It supports projects which either improve areas for nature, or make them more accessible, so that local people can visit, understand and enjoy wildlife in their area, and be more aware of the surrounding countryside. Biodiversity grants are available to landowners or groups for small-scale biodiversity projects and are intended to support projects that enhance or create important habitats or undertake work to increase the number of important species.

The Organic Option

In November 2007 the National Assembly launched the new, revised Organic Farming Scheme, aimed at helping farmers and growers interested in converting to organic production. Support and guidance is available for farmers wishing to consider organic conversion, through the Organic Conversion Information Service (OCIS). The Organic Conversion Information Service is free and funded by the National Assembly. It provides telephone advice, an information pack and on-site advisory visits. Advisers will explain the organic standards, assess different aspects of the farm and outline the sources of help available. Advice is given on the key elements of conversion planning, as well as topics like pest and disease control, crop rotations, marketing and applying for grants. About 90 per cent of farms achieve conversion within two years.

Consumer demand for organic food has grown rapidly over the past decade and continues to do so, particularly in the wake of the various disease crises in UK agriculture and following high-profile campaigns by celebrity chefs like Jamie Oliver, Hugh Fearnley-Whittingstall and Gordon Ramsay. DEFRA says that retail sales of organic produce are now worth approx. £1.2bn a year. Conversion is certainly something to consider if you're looking at niche market products. There are more than 4,600 organic and in-conversion producers in the UK. Of those, 15.3 per cent are based in Wales. Wales has the highest percentage of organic and in-conversion land (5.5 per cent) as a proportion of the total land of the UK.

The term 'organic', when applied to food, has a legal meaning. It means the food has been grown and processed according to certain standards, which are legally enforceable in the UK and across Europe. These standards cover every stage of organic food production, from farm to shop. To be able to call yourself an organic producer, you have to be registered with one of the organic accreditation organizations, details of which are below.

With regard to livestock, they must have enough room to express their natural behaviour; all stock must have access to pasture when conditions allow; intensive feeding of beef and dairy cattle and the use of battery hen cages is not allowed; no routine dosing with antibiotics is permitted. Crops must be raised naturally, which means cultivation concentrates on rotation – growing different crops in the same area in consecutive seasons to avoid build-up of pests and diseases. Very few artificial fertilizers are allowed; instead, farmers increase soil fertility by digging in clover and animal manure. Organic farmers are only allowed to use a small number of pesticides, and even then only under certain conditions. No herbicides are permitted.

There are, of course, drawbacks to farming organically. Labour costs can be high and yields are generally lower than on non-organic farms. Organically grown feed for animals can be costly and difficult to source. Processed organic foods can be more expensive than conventional equivalents because the cost of ingredients is higher. In addition to all this, the cost of getting certified by one of the recognized organic bodies can be expensive. The knock-on effect of high production costs is a higher price for the consumer, which can be off-putting. However, shoppers are slowly coming to realize the benefits of organic food and more and more are now willing to pay the higher prices.

FURTHER INFORMATION

NFU Cymru, Agriculture House, Royal Welsh Showground, Builth Wells, Powys LD2 3TU, tel. 01982 554200, fax 01982 554201 (*www.nfu-cymru.org.uk*).

Farmers' Union of Wales, Llys Amaeth, Plas Gogerddan, Aberystwyth SY23 3BT, tel. 01970 820820, fax 01970 820821 (*www.fuw.org.uk*).

Organic Centre Wales, Institute of Rural Sciences,University of Wales Aberystwyth,
Ceredigion, Y23 3AL, tel: 01970 622248, fax: 01970 622238 (*www.organic.aber.ac.uk*).

DEFRA, for general information on organic systems, converting to organic farming, news and
statistics (*www.defra.gov.uk/farm/organic*).

Centre for Organic Seed, organic and non-organic seed suppliers, plus information on how
standards are developing in the UK and Europe (*www.cosi.org.uk*).

Wholesome Food Association (an alternative to organic certification which provides a
low-cost labelling scheme for marketing wholesome, locally grown food), Ball Cottage,
East Ball Hill, Hartland, Devon EX39 6BU, tel. 01237 441 118 (*www.wholesome-food.org.uk*).

7

LEGAL REQUIREMENTS

ELCOME TO the world of red tape! You don't have to register your property as a smallholding – but you do if you want to keep most livestock. If you only want to keep poultry on a small scale, there is nothing to oblige you to tell anyone, though you do need to contact the Great Britain Poultry Register if you keep more than fifty birds at any time during the year. However, if you want to venture into keeping four-legged livestock, even as pets, you need to go through a slightly cumbersome – but necessary – process.

Step 1: Get your CPH

First you have to get yourself a County/Parish/Holding number (CPH). It will look something like mine: 58/421/0086. The first two digits are the county, the next three the parish in which you live, and the final four the actual number of your holding. You will need to use this number whenever you buy or sell livestock, move animals on or off your premises, when ordering identification tags and in numerous official documents at some time or another. Getting one is normally straightforward. Just contact the relevant Welsh Assembly Government

Doris, proud mother, and her new-born lamb.

office – whichever of the following is nearest to you. All it takes is a phone call and staff will send you a form to fill out. It doesn't take long; I got my number within a fortnight of picking up the phone.

North Wales
Caernarfon Divisional Office, tel. 01286 674144,
    e-mail: agriculture.caernarfon@wales.gsi.gov.uk

Mid- and south-east Wales
Llandrindod Walls Divisional Office, tel. 01597 823777,
    e-mail: agriculture.llandrindod@wales.gsi.gov.uk

West Wales
Carmarthen Divisional Office, tel. 01267 225300,
    e-mail: agriculture.carmarthen@wales.gsi.gov.uk

Step 2: Get a Flock and/or Herd Number

All livestock-keepers are treated the same, even if their animals are kept as pets. Bizarrely, there is no such thing as a one-stop shop when it comes to getting registered to keep livestock. I've no idea why the process needs to be so complicated and time-consuming, involving so many different people, but I expect some civil servant could come up with a whole host of reasons. Anyway, once you've got your CPH number, as explained above, you need to get a flock/herd number for sheep, goats or cattle (all the same number), and a herd number for pigs. This number will come from your nearest Animal Health Divisional Office (AHDO). There are three AHDOs, run by Welsh Assembly Government staff on behalf of the Department for Environment, Food and Rural Affairs (DEFRA):

Caernarfon tel. 01286 674144, e-mail: ah.caernarfon@animalhealth.gsi.gov.uk

Cardiff tel. 029 2076 8500, e-mail: ah.cardiff@animalhealth.gsi.gov.uk

Carmarthen tel. 01267 245400, e-mail: ah.carmarthen@animalhealth.gsi.gov.uk

Step 3: Identification and Tagging

Once you have your flock and/or herd number, you will be able to order identification tags for your animals. Whichever company you choose will ask you for your CPH and your flock/herd numbers.

Sheep and goats

Sheep and goats born on your holding used to require just one ID tag, but new EU legislation introduced in January 2008 means that any which are *not* intended for slaughter now have to be double-tagged. This only affects animals born after 11 January 2008. In practice, this means that animals which you intend to keep for breeding must be double-tagged. If, however, you originally intend to fatten a sheep or a goat for meat, but then decide to keep it for breeding, a second tag – or a tattoo – must be added. This has to be done before the animal is 12 months old. DEFRA recommends one tag in each ear (or one tag and one tattoo), or one tag in the left ear in the case of those requiring just a single tag.

Keepers must inspect sheep and goats for signs of foot-and-mouth disease before movement. Any signs must be notified to the Divisional Veterinary Manager (DVM) of the local Animal Health Divisional Office. All sheep, goat and deer movements must be accompanied by a completed animal movement licence (AML1). There are four copies – one white, one pink, one blue and one yellow – and details must be completed by both the departure premises (i.e. where the animals were kept) and the destination premises. The person receiving the animals must send the white copy to the trading standards department of his or her local authority within three days of the movement taking place. The pink copy is kept by the person receiving the animals, the blue copy is for the haulier and the yellow copy is kept by the departure premises. Any movement of sheep onto your land triggers a six-day 'standstill' – which means nothing can leave your holding until that time is up.

All sheep and goat keepers are obliged to keep a flock/herd register which contains details of animals kept on the holding, movements on and off, births and deaths. These details can be kept in a book (the National Assembly produces free copies, or similar books can be bought from agricultural suppliers, and trading standards departments will normally supply sheets for you to fill in) or stored on a computer. In addition, the Welsh Assembly Government operates an Annual Sheep and Goat Inventory. All keepers are sent a form which must be completed with details of how many animals they currently have.

Pigs

Any pigs less than a year old can be moved from one holding to another with just a temporary paint mark on their backs. Older pigs need to be identified with a herdmark from each holding they depart – either a tag, a tattoo or a slapmark on the shoulder. In practice, you don't have to tag pigs until they leave your holding. If they are going for slaughter, the ear tag bearing your herd number must be heat-resistant – sufficiently strong to withstand the abattoir process without melting – so metal tags are normally used.

The animal movement document (AML2) which must accompany any pig movement is almost the same as the one for sheep, goats, and deer. However, there is a small additional section which asks the person receiving the pigs about their condition on arrival. As with sheep, goats and deer, the white copy is for trading standards, and has to be sent within three days, the pink is for the destination premises, blue is for the haulier and yellow copy the departure premises. Pig movements onto your premises trigger a twenty-day standstill.

All pig keepers must keep a movement record book, similar to the one for sheep and goats, which again contains details of animals kept on the holding, movements on and off, births and deaths. Trading standards will normally be able to supply sheets for you to fill in and file, or record books can be bought from agricultural suppliers.

Cattle

All cattle born after 1 January 1998, must have an eartag in each ear, both bearing the same herd number. The primary tag – which can be in either ear – is yellow plastic and has the British 'crown' logo and the unique ID number. The secondary tag – in the other ear – can be plastic or metal and must carry the information included on the primary tag.

Any cattle born since 1 July 1996 must also have a cattle passport – a document which confirms identification details (sex, breed, date of birth, identification of the mother) and records its movement history. When you buy cattle, each animal must have its own passport. If they were born after 28 September 1998, this will be a 'cheque book'-style passport issued by the British Cattle Movement Service (BCMS). Older animals will have registration certificates issued by the BCMS. These documents are part of the Cattle Tracing System administered by the BCMS and are designed to trace cattle quickly in the event of a disease outbreak. The passport (or the registration certificate) stays with the animal, and when it is moved the document is passed onto the new keeper, who sends it to the BCMS for updating. The standstill period for cattle is the same as for sheep – six days.

If cattle are born on your holding, you will need to apply for a passport to the BCMS. When you apply for eartags you will automatically be sent an application form which will be pre-printed with the eartag number and details of your premises. This must be completed and sent to BCMS before your calf is twenty-seven days old. Details of all births and movements between holdings, markets and abattoirs, must be notified to the central Cattle Tracing System (CTS) computer database run by the BCMS, part of the Rural Payments Agency (RPA). Unlike pigs and sheep, there is no contact with the local authority trading standards department.

Cattle keepers must also keep an up-to-date, accurate herd register of the cattle on their holding, recording identification numbers, breed and sex, dates of births, deaths and movements on and off their farms, together with details of where the cattle came from or went to, and the identification of the mother.

Transportation of Livestock

Everyone transporting livestock has to ensure that journey times are kept to a minimum; that the animals are fit to travel; that those handling the animals are competent;

that the vehicle and its loading and unloading facilities are designed, constructed and maintained to avoid injury and suffering; that water, feed and rest are provided as necessary; that there is sufficient space. A new EU regulation governing the welfare of animals during transport came into force in January 2007. Now, anyone transporting animals more than 65km (40 miles) in connection with an economic activity needs to apply for a transporter authorization, which is granted by the State Veterinary Service and is valid for five years.

The regulation is relevant to livestock and equine hauliers, farmers and commercial pet breeders, as well as people working at markets and abattoirs. You are only affected if the movement is being carried out as part of a business or commercial activity. Exemptions include: transportation of animals not in connection with an economic activity; transportation to or from veterinary practices under veterinary advice; journeys involving a single animal, accompanied by its owner or other responsible person; 'hobby breeders' whose income does not exceed the expenses of the hobby; journeys where the animals are pets accompanied by their owner; farmers transporting their own animals, in their own vehicles, under 50km.

There are two types of authorization – one for short journeys (more than 65km and up to eight hours long), and one for longer journeys (more than eight hours). In addition to the standard welfare rules regarding transportation outlined above, anyone moving stock over 65km must now hold a transporter authorization, ensure that drivers and attendants transporting horses, farmed animals or poultry have a certificate of competence; show they have appropriate staff and equipment to move animals in a proper way; show that they have no record of seriously infringing animal welfare legislation in the past three years; complete an Animal Transport Certificate for each journey. Anyone carrying out longer journeys must have the long journey transporter authorization, must have the vehicle inspected and approved for transporting horses or farmed animals, have contingency plans in case of an emergency; and, if the animals are travelling beyond the UK, ensure the journey log has been completed.

Veterinary Medicine Records

If you keep animals for food production, you must keep a record of any veterinary medicines administered. Record must be kept for three years and be available for inspection on request. Where prescriptions are used as the record they must be kept for five years and the actual dates of administration of the treatment must be noted.

Trading standards departments will supply forms for you to fill in and file, or you can store records on computer. The kind of details required include the date the medicine was purchased, its name, batch ID and quantity purchased; the name and address of the supplier; the dates treatment started and finished; the date the withdrawal period ended; ID numbers of animals treated; the total quantity used; and the name of the person who administered the medicine.

8

YOUR FIRST LIVESTOCK

Introduction

BECOMING A LANDOWNER for the first time is such a thrilling experience, it's easy to let your excitement run away with you. There's a natural temptation to rush out and buy some livestock to fill those empty fields. Just imagine how lovely it would be to gaze out of your bedroom window and see fluffy white sheep or a few spotted pigs grazing contentedly! But hang on a minute – have you thought of the practicalities? Ask yourself these questions before you go too far along a route which may be the wrong one for you.

Why Do I Want to Own Livestock?

Is the aim to produce meat, do you just want animals in the fields to keep the grass down, or do you just want them to enhance the landscape? There are alternatives to owning livestock; unless you want to raise your own animals for meat, you might be better off renting out your fields for grazing, so that you get the benefit of having animals around, while someone else has the responsibility and the expense of looking after them.

Am I Sufficiently Competent to Look After Livestock?

Have you the necessary knowledge or training to care for the animals you want? Have you done your homework and found out what husbandry is involved? Are you physically fit enough to cope with the task ahead? What would happen if you fell ill or had an accident? Are you really committed enough to go trudging through muddy fields in all weathers to complete the necessary chores? What would you do in an emergency? Does the local vet treat farm animals? Find out, because many don't.

Am I Emotionally Prepared for Keeping Livestock?

As that old saying goes, 'Where there's livestock, there's deadstock'. Chances are, you will have to deal with illness, injury and death. Could you, for instance, humanely kill an animal if you had to? Something may need putting out of its misery, with no one else around to do it.

Do I Have the Land and Buildings that I Need?
It's easy to underestimate how much grazing you will need, so talk to people with experience before committing yourself. Even if you want your livestock to be completely free-range, you must offer shelter from extreme weather conditions; hot summer sun can be just as bad as harsh winter weather. Similarly, you should have a barn or shed available in case of illness, or for overwintering stock, should the ground become too waterlogged or need resting. Don't forget you'll also need somewhere secure to house feed and bedding. It's surprising how much you'll go through.

Are my Boundary Fences up to Scratch?
Never trust to luck. Fences and hedges have to be secure – for the protection of your livestock, to protect neighbours' land and property, and for the safety of passers-by. You should also consider finding an insurance policy which covers not only your livestock, but also third-party damage.

Being a Responsible Owner: the Five Freedoms

The welfare of animals has to be the most important consideration, whatever livestock you choose to keep. This section of the book has been written as an introduction for new smallholders who care not only about the quality of the food they intend to produce, but also about the quality of life their animals will be given. There are five 'freedoms' to which livestock should be entitled:

Freedom from hunger and thirst: animals must have ready access to fresh water and a diet to maintain full health and vigour.
Freedom from discomfort: they should have an appropriate environment, including shelter and a comfortable resting area.
Freedom from pain, injury, or disease: appropriate care should be given to prevent health problems, and there should be rapid diagnosis and treatment.
Freedom to express normal behaviour: there should be sufficient space, proper facilities, and animals should have the company of others of the same species.
Freedom from fear and distress: mental suffering must be prevented by ensuring animals must live in appropriate conditions and are given appropriate treatment.

The DEFRA website (*www.defra.gov.uk*) has excellent guides to the welfare of all farm animals. Look in the 'Animal Health and Welfare' section, then click on 'Animal Welfare', then 'On-Farm Animal Welfare'. Alternatively, ring them on on 08459 335577 to request hard copies. The Welsh Assembly Government's Environment, Planning and

Countryside department website (*www.countryside.wales.gov.uk*) also has an Animal Health and Welfare section, which includes downloadable advice on welfare and legal requirements.

Getting some training

If you're considering keeping anything other than poultry, I would strongly advise getting some training in basic care and handling. You'll find more on this subject in Chapter 5.

As you may remember from earlier in the book, both Gerry and myself were complete beginners when it came to looking after anything other than household pets. I was determined to learn about livestock before I went and bought any animals, and I was fortunate that Pencoed College – just forty minutes down the motorway – was running a course for smallholders.

It was money really well-spent. The twelve-week course covered all the basics with regard to sheep, pigs, cattle and goats. As the college had its own farm at the time (facilities which, unfortunately, have since been sold off), we had access to live animals and expert tuition from tutors who lived on working farms and were also excellent communicators.

Administering treatment for the first time is a lot easier when you do it under supervision, and watching an old hand performing a procedure is much better than trying to learn from pictures in books.

Buying your first livestock

As well as doing your homework before making any purchases, the other absolutely essential thing I would recommend is that you only buy from reputable breeders. It's just common sense; good breeders sell good stock, free from disease or deformity, and won't take you for a ride because you're new to the game. A one-to-one transaction, carried out on a farm, rather than at a market filled with lots of other livestock, is also much less risky from a health point of view. Word-of-mouth recommendations are worth their weight in gold. Ask around locally and find out who rears what. Alternatively, if you're interested in a particular breed, check out the breed society websites, which will normally have contact details.

When you're buying your smallholding, the vendor might well offer to sell you some or all of the resident livestock. Unless you have the necessary experience, or feel the vendor is particularly honest and helpful, it's best to seek advice from someone who knows about livestock and can assess their health and market value. Don't necessarily think you'll be getting a bargain; most animals are fairly cheap to buy, so don't be rushed into becoming a livestock-keeper before you're good and ready.

Buying at auction

Another thing to be wary of until you've got a bit of experience under your belt is buying at auction. Auctions are great fun and extremely exciting, but they are riddled with pitfalls for the novice buyer. You have to know exactly what you're proposing to buy, and be able to carry out all the basic health checks before bidding. Would you know, for instance, how to tell the age of a sheep? Could you tell if a sow's teats would support a full litter? Do you know foot rot when you see it or smell it?

The other big danger is that it is all too easy to get carried away and bid on something you don't really need, or to get locked in a bidding war with another novice, so the price is pushed up to an unrealistic level. Having said all that, auctions are brilliant entertainment, and there's nothing like going home, safe in the knowledge that you've snapped up a real bargain – even if it is stinking out the back of the car and creating a deafening racket. So, if you are going to take a gamble at an auction, there are a few things you should bear in mind.

1. Go to as a visitor first. Learn about the way auctions work – for example, how to register and get your bidder's number, how much commission you'll to pay on top, methods of payment accepted, when you can collect your purchases.

2. Work out what equipment/vehicle you'll need to transport your animals home. Remember that you won't necessarily be given a cardboard box for your chickens, as breeders tend to bring their birds in cages or crates which they take home with them. The last thing you want is loose birds or other animals running amok in the back of the car.

3. If you know an auction is coming up, contact the organizers for a copy of the catalogue. This will give you time to see what's going to be on offer, then you can check the current market prices and do some research on any breeds you're not familiar with.

4. Take someone knowledgeable with you. You can't beat the advice of someone who has experience of buying and rearing the type of animal you've set your sights on.

5. Arrive early. Note which lots you're interested in and give yourself plenty of time to have a good look at the livestock, and make sure it's what you really want to buy. Turn up when the auction is just about to start, and you'll be straining your neck to see what's being sold. Also, you'll need to get registered and collect your buyer's number before you can start bidding.

6. Check how many animals are being sold in each lot. In poultry auctions, for instance, the auctioneer may offer six birds for sale, but the bids will be *per bird*, rather than for the whole lot. If you win, you'll have the option of buying some or all of the birds at the winning price.

7. When you're taking a look at an animal before the auction, make sure it's fit and healthy. Never buy anything which looks too quiet, or generally under the weather, thinking it will be much better when you get it home. Basic things to watch for include:

- General appearance and posture – listlessness, dull eyes, droopy head, dry muzzle, reluctance to stand
- Discharge from eyes or nose; scouring (i.e. diarrhoea)
- Generally poor coat/skin – dull or scruffy hair or feathers, bald spots, scabs; animal scratching a lot

- Coughing or sneezing – could indicate respiratory problems
- Lameness or other signs suggesting the animal is in pain
- Lumps in udders, suggesting mastitis
- Poor or missing teeth, which could cause feeding problems

8. Make sure in advance that you have accommodation ready for whatever you buy. You don't want to have to keep animals cooped up for hours in a vehicle or trailer while you get their new home ready.

For more general advice on buying at auctions, see Chapter 5.

Eating your own

I think it's worth mentioning at this stage that not everyone who starts off rearing live-stock actually ends up putting meat on the table. If I had a pound for every smallhold-er I've met with 'pet' sheep and pigs in residence, I wouldn't be working for a living now. A lot of people like the *idea* of raising their own meat, but when it comes to D-Day (D for death, of course), they can't bring themselves to pronounce sentence. Quite simply, you have to think long and hard about this before you make any commitments.

Liz's dog Gordon with Thumper, a ram lamb who was destined to become chops.

It took me two years of smallholding before I started thinking about rearing live-stock for the table. Prior to that, it was just hens for eggs and ducks for decoration. Then, one day, we were at a poultry auction, looking for more chickens, we saw three young turkeys which we thought would be good to raise for Christmas. I would be lying if I said that eating a home-reared turkey that first time was easy. I wandered around for hours beforehand feeling like Lady Macbeth, wringing my hands – but in the end he did taste lovely. Within a short space of time, I became a fully paid-up member of the 'eat your own' club, even if I did feel a bit like one of those people in the vampire films who had just taken the first bite of forbidden flesh. In a way, I was glad when it was over, but I knew I would do it again. I've been a meat-eater for most of my life, apart from a brief spell in my troubled, idealistic teens, so it would have been highly hypocritical had I refused to eat the perfectly good turkey we had raised. One consolation was knowing its life was good while it lasted.

Giving the birds their final feed on Sunday wasn't made easier by the fact that Gerry was sizing them all up and lifting them to see which one should grace our table. There I was, making sure they all got some fresh greens, and there was Gerry, looking for the biggest bird. When we sat down to lunch on Christmas Day I did have a few fleeting flashes of Banquo's ghost, but they soon passed when the wine came round.

Whatever you plan to start rearing, you have to think about the end of the process, too. Animals have to be slaughtered humanely and, if they are for anyone other than yourself, they need to be killed at a licensed abattoir. As we discovered, abattoirs in Wales are few and far between. Fortunately, we found one in the end – after a lot of phoning round – but, depending on where you live, you may have a more difficult job, so get everything organized in plenty of time. The Food Standards Agency (tel. 029 20678999 or *www.food.gov.uk*) has a list of licensed premises, and produces a range of publications with advice on food production. Go to the home page and look for the link which says 'Food industries'.

If you're planning to kill a bird for your own consumption, do find out how to do it properly. The Humane Slaughter Association (*www.hsa.org.uk* or ring 01582 831919) is an excellent source of information. It produces a range of publications – including *Practical Slaughter of Poultry: A Guide for the Small Producer* – all available by mail order. There is also a video – not for the squeamish, I should warn you – which shows exactly how animals should be humanely killed.

The following section is not intended to be an exhaustive guide to choosing and caring for livestock, but simply as an introduction to the kind of animals you might consider keeping on your smallholding. At the end of each section you will see a list of recommended reading, plus contacts for organizations run by people with far more in-depth knowledge of each species mentioned than I could ever hope to have.

Please take your time before committing to buy livestock and – I know I keep saying this, but it is important – do your homework before taking the plunge.

Birds

Recent outbreaks of avian influenza have changed the rules and regulations regarding keeping poultry and other birds. Although there is still no requirement for poultry-keepers to have a County/Parish/Holding number, anyone with more than fifty birds MUST supply their details to the Great Britain Poultry Register. This applies even if – like a lot of people who rear poultry for the Christmas or Easter market – your birds only reach fifty at certain times of the year. Those with smaller flocks do not have to register, but DEFRA, the Welsh Assembly Government and the Scottish Executive, are encouraging them to do so.

The birds covered by the register are chickens, ducks, geese, turkeys, partridges, guinea fowl, quail, pigeons, pheasants, emus, rheas and ostriches. DEFRA has an advice line for queries – ring the main number (08459 335577) and choose the avian flu option. Or see the website (*poultry.defra.gov.uk* – note there is no 'www.' prefix). Poultry-keepers are not bound by the kind of movement rules which apply to those who farm other animals. You can buy or sell a bird without having to fill in movement documents and without informing your local trading standards people.

No one who keeps poultry is complacent about the risks posed by avian flu, but you have to keep it in perspective – particularly as certain sections of the media switch immediately into end-of-the-world mode when a case is diagnosed. Don't panic! In order to be infected, you first need to be suffering from human flu (and not just a cold or the sniffles), and you have to be in *extremely* close contact with an affected bird – closer than any poultry-keepers in the UK would ever get. Avian flu can't be caught from eating eggs or poultry meat. You would have to ingest faeces, saliva or mucus from a bird at the infectious stage. How likely is that? Eating eggs and properly cooked poultry meat poses no threat, so bon appétit!

Certain birds, including swans, muscovy ducks and geese, are regarded as 'sentinel' birds with no resistance to avian flu, and are early indicators of problems. More than one death should be reported, using the DEFRA number. Dead birds should be carefully bagged, and care taken to avoid contact. Hands and clothes which come into contact with the carcasses should be thoroughly washed as soon as possible.

The Welsh Assembly Government website says that, although the risk of avian influenza is low, birds can carry other respiratory infections. Birds can also carry infections which can cause gastrointestinal infections such as salmonella and campylobacter.

The Environment, Planning and Countryside Committee website (*www.countryside.wales.gov.uk*) has information on protecting your birds from avian flu, which includes basic biosecurity advice and separating your flock from wild birds. The most sensible advice anyone can give, however, is to practise good husbandry, be observant and know your birds, and act quickly and correctly should you spot anything unusual.

Protecting your stock

Don't underestimate foxes! Your birds must be kept in a safe run or enclosure, otherwise, sooner or later, you're going to get a nasty surprise. We lost fifty in one attack thanks to our own negligence. Most foxes will patrol their territory at all times of the day, and the increasing trend for well-meaning folk to feed foxes in their back gardens in towns and cities means that today's fox is far less afraid of humans and much more cocky and opportunistic. From the big massacre, three years ago, we learned that foxes are far more likely to dig *under* a fence than try to climb over it. Our hens are as free-range as they can be with foxes around. They have plenty of room to roam around their paddock, scratch for insects and enjoy dust baths. They let themselves in and out of their house, but the paddock in which the house sits is surrounded by strong, 2" Weldmesh wire, reaching 4ft high. To make it fox-proof, we attached a kind of 'skirt' of this same wire to the bottom of the fence, which we then buried under stones and earth. As this 2ft extension sat on the ground, it eventually got knitted tightly in place by grass. When the fox approaches the edge of the fence and starts digging, he hits the wire, realizes he's getting nowhere, and gives up. We don't have any badgers in our area, but this system would probably be enough of a deterrent if we did.

There are some other methods of deterring predators which have been recommended to me, but I've not tried. Human hair clippings scattered around the fence, or placed in carrier bags tied to it, are supposed to be a deterrent. Human urine, too, has been suggested, but Gerry didn't fancy that one, for some reason. Llamas are supposed to scare foxes, because they instinctively defend their 'herd' – whatever animals it might contain – but I've not been allowed to have one so far.

It's all very well stopping predators from getting in, but if a bird insists on getting out, it's just as likely to become a takeaway meal. Unless you want to build a prison-height fence, wing-clipping is the answer. This involves snipping off the flight – or primary – feathers of one wing. Only one wing is done, so that it unbalances the bird, making flying impossible. Get someone with experience to show you how it's done, or ask your vet for advice if you don't feel sufficiently confident. Clipping is a painless procedure – a bit like trimming nails – but you have to be careful not to cut too far up the shaft of the feather or you'll draw blood. If this happens, keep the bird separate from the others for a few minutes, until the bleeding stops. Clean away any blood before returning it to the flock, otherwise it might be attacked.

Make sure you only trim the primary feathers – the others are for insulation. Bear in mind, too, that you'll have to repeat the process after the birds moult, because the feathers will regrow.

Chickens have an inquisitive nature. Luckily Bryn doesn't mind.

Chickens

Ask most newcomers to smallholding what's at the top of the shopping list, and 99 per cent will say chickens. They're really easy to keep, don't demand any great animal husbandry skills and they're also entertaining and rewarding. Once you've got them settled in, they will give you eggs which knock spots of any you'll buy in a supermarket – and all you have to do in return is provide food, water and a clean and dry place for them to live.

Although raising chickens from day-old chicks, or even eggs, can be a cheap way of getting a flock, it does need some skill, time, and specialist brooding equipment, and mortality rates can be disappointingly high. Instead, I recommend buying young hens which are almost ready to lay (described as 'point of lay' pullets), about 18 to 20 weeks old.

Choosing breeds

The type of birds you choose will depend on the space you have available, whether you need them to provide both eggs and meat, and your own personal preferences. Getting to see the variety of birds on offer is always a good idea. Farmers' marts and specialist poultry fairs are held across Wales on a regular basis, and provide the ideal opportunity to view different breeds and talk to the breeders. Events like the Royal Welsh Smallholder and Garden Festival, held at Llanelwedd, Builth Wells, every May, is an excellent place to start. The website of the Poultry Club of Great Britain (*www.poultryclub.org* or 01476 550067) is also a good place for information on breeds and suppliers, as well as guidance on handling and caring for birds. See below for more website links.

Most of the popular breeds have bantam varieties – minature versions – so if space is an issue, bantams could be the answer. They lay smaller eggs, but also eat less, so cost less to keep. Easy to handle, they are a good choice if children are to be involved in the rearing process. Be warned, though – bantams tend to get broody much more often than standard-sized birds, so make sure you collect the eggs several times a day to stop any maternal feelings developing.

I always like to have a mixed flock because I like seeing different varieties all living together, and I also like the variety in the colour of the eggs I collect. Always buy in your birds at the same time, if you can, to reduce the risk of fighting, and choose similar-sized breeds.

I have described some of my own favourite breeds below.

Araucana
These lay the coveted blue-green eggs favoured by supermarkets at the higher end of the scale. The blue gene is dominant, so is carried on even if the birds are cross-bred. Araucanas are fairly small birds, but can be raised for meat. They come in various colours, with the most popular shade being lavender – which is a really nice silvery-grey.

Black rock
A hardy, good-laying hybrid, created by crossing a Rhode Island red with a Barred Plymouth Rock (female line). Docile and easy to handle, they have thick plumage – either black with a green sheen or black and golden brown – and lay medium-brown eggs for a surprisingly long time, sometimes as long as ten years.

Buff Orpington
This is what I call the Golden Retriever of the chicken world. It has handsome, dense, straw-berry-blond plumage and lays brown eggs. An extremely attractive addition to any flock, and even lovelier in a garden.

Light Sussex
One of the oldest breeds in the UK, this large bird is easily recognizable with its white body, black 'cloak' of shoulder feathers and black tail. Suitable for both eggs and meat, it is a good bet for all climates.

Maran
The French Maran is a favourite with many because of its ability to supply both eggs and meat, but also because it produces the most wonderful chocolate-brown eggs in good quantities. The most common variety is the Cuckoo Maran, with black and white speckled plumage.

Rhode Island red
Another hybrid created for eggs and meat, this American bird is probably the best of the dual-purpose breeds. Fairly hardy, they have deep reddish-brown feathers. *(continued)*

Welsummer

The male of this Dutch breed is the archetypal handsome farmyard cockerel – the sort you see immortalized in ornaments and on cereal packets. Welsummer hens are attractive, too, with brown plumage which changes from gold at the neck to dark brown at the tail. They lay large, dark-brown eggs.

First hens

Gerry and I started timidly, with half a dozen birds, all bought at point of lay. You can, of course, buy birds which are already laying well, but you'll find that egg production slows down after the first year – which is why you see so many classified ad 'bargains' offering layers for sale.

As mentioned earlier, you can buy day-old chicks and rear them under an infra-red lamp until they are fully feathered. This is extremely satisfying but time-consuming and, as many chicks die in the first few days, it can also be upsetting. If you do decide to go down this route (Katie Thear's *Starting with Chickens* explains how and is an excellent reference guide), and you want hens for eggs, make sure the chicks have been sexed first – otherwise you may end up, like we did once, with nine unwanted cockerels out of a dozen chicks.

When you get your hens home, give them time to settle. We shut new birds in for the first day and night, so they grow accustomed to their new surroundings. They have food and water inside until they are ready to brave the great outdoors – which isn't long, once they realize what grass tastes like. Our first hens came from a commercial breeder and, like a lot of shed-reared birds, were used to dark, cramped conditions, so their new accommodation must have been like a five-star hotel. With hindsight, we gave them

Warrens are used in intensive egg production but adapt quickly to the free-range lifestyle.

more coop space they needed. As a general rule of thumb, each bird needs about eight inches (20cm) of perch space, with the lowest perch about two feet (60cm) off the ground. If you're buying a purpose-built house, it'll probably have ready-made nest boxes, so sleeping and laying areas are kept separate, meaning less chance of dirty or broken eggs. You can always adapt a large rabbit hutch or a garden tool shed into a suitable home, making sure there is sufficient ventilation, and providing boxes for laying.

Bedding is a matter of choice – we use straw, but others prefer woodshavings or shredded newspapers; some choose to have slatted bases to their coops so droppings fall straight through, but I don't think this is a particularly bird-friendly system. We've always fed our birds on good-quality layers' pellets and occasional mixed corn – both easily available from your local feed merchant. With plenty of grass available, you won't need to feed more than once a day. Don't feed your birds more than they can clear in five minutes, or you'll just be feeding the local wildlife – as our local magpies learned quickly. And don't forget the importance of water – you'll be surprised how much chickens drink.

Cockerels

People often ask me whether they should keep a cockerel, quoting the ridiculous old wives' tale that hens lay better in the presence of a male. Unless you want to start breeding, there really is no point (and even if you do, what would you do with all the unwanted male chicks you would inevitably get?). My opinion is that cockerels are more trouble than they're worth. They pester the hens mercilessly, stressing them out so much that they actually lay less, and they rip feathers out in the heat of mating. They can be aggressive to their owners, too. I know people will disagree with me, but cockerels get a massive thumbs-down where I'm concerned. Chances are, your neighbours won't like them, either.

Health problems

Most poultry-keepers with small, free-range flocks will never have any problem with serious infectious diseases. If you buy your chickens from a good breeder, they will probably have been vaccinated (unless sold as organic) against the most commonly seen problems, Marek's disease, Newcastle disease and infectious bronchitis. Commercial birds have been tested for salmonella, too.

Good husbandry is the key to keeping your birds healthy, so regular cleaning and disinfecting of chicken houses is a must. This minimizes the risk of respiratory diseases spreading and, when combined with regular dusting using an appropriate insecticide, lessens the risk of external parasites.

Some common problems you may encounter include scaly leg (caused by a small parasite burrowing under the scales), mites and lice, and internal worms. All of these conditions are easily treatable, so don't worry, but inspect your flock regularly and stay vigilant.

Getting advice

Of course, no one should rush into buying any kind of animal without doing some homework first. You really should get a good book on the subject – something like

Starting with Chickens by Katie Thear – which will be a useful reference manual that you'll keep going back to. Katie's book is one of the best on the market, and affordable, but some books on poultry-keeping can be expensive, so it's well worth surfing the internet for free advice – often provided by people so caught up in the whole chicken-keeping thing that they can't wait to pass on their knowledge to others. See below for more useful books and website addresses.

Ducks

Pretty little ducks, dabbling about on a pond, occasionally wandering ashore to pick troublesome slugs from the vegetable patch; gentle quacks in the distance, adding to the aural delight that is the soundtrack to the countryside experience. Or maybe not.

I really like ducks, but I know from bitter experience that they are messy, destructive, noisy creatures. Don't buy any until you've talked to and, preferably, visited someone who has some already. The trouble with ducks is that, entertaining as they are, they tend to devour everything in sight. We dug out a wildlife pond about a year before getting our first ducklings. All was well until they started to grow and investigate their new sur-roundings. Within weeks, all visible signs of vegetation on the banks had disappeared and only bare clay and muddy water remained. And we ended up with too many drakes chasing too few females. Before long, we decided to sell the lot.

Okay, so that's the bad news, but you had to have it. Ducks can, indeed, be delightful creatures. They are, in my opinion, more attractive and more entertaining than chickens, and a lot less labour-intensive. They aren't fussy eaters, surviving quite contentedly on standard chicken feed and they don't suffer from as many ailments as hens. Many breeds lay far more eggs, and they lay first thing in the morning, so there's no trekking back and forth to check on deliveries. If you're a keen gardener, they can be powerful aides in the battle against slugs and snails – as long as you don't mind losing a few plants.

It can be a real temptation to buy ducklings, but they will need extra care until their feathers become waterproof.

Choosing breeds

All but one of today's popular breeds are descended from the wild mallard. The exception is the muscovy, which originated from central and south America. Mallards are thought to have been domesticated in Egyptian times and, until Victorian times, ducks were kept primarily for meat rather than eggs. Today, many people – particularly keen bakers – prize the bigger, richer ducks' eggs far above those of hens. Everyone has their personal preferences, but some of the most popular are listed in the box opposite.

Aylesbury
Originally called the White English, this large, white bird gets its name from the Vale of Aylesbury. Fast-growing, so cheap to raise for meat.

Blue Swedish
This is one of my personal favourites – a large, striking bird with blue-grey plumage, black head, and white bib. Eggs are tinted blue or green.

Call ducks
Probably the least destructive of all ducks, because of their small size and habits. However, be warned – they are immensely noisy, with an often irritating, high-pitched call, which is why hunters use them to lure in wild ducks. They come in lots of different colours and varieties, so there's sure to be one to suit your tastes.

Cayuga
A US breed with the most amazing plumage – black with an irridescent green sheen. A large breed, it is popular for both meat and eggs.

Indian runner
These are the 'wine bottles' of the duck world – thin and upright, with long necks. If you've visited a big agricultural show, you may have seen Meirion and his Quack Pack – the shepherd who trains runners to behave like sheepdogs. Runners are excellent layers, and great entertainment, but too skinny for meat.

Khaki campbell
One of the most popular choices for commercial egg producers. Created by crossing Indian runner, mallard and Rouen, it's a small brown-feathered bird producing white eggs on an astonishingly regular basis.

Muscovy
You either love them or you hate them. I think they're incredibly ugly, thanks to the bright red 'mask' around the eyes and on top of the beak. They are big, strong birds, and their feet have claws – designed to help them climb trees – which makes handling them a bit dangerous. They don't swim a lot, because their oil glands aren't as efficient as other ducks.

Rouen
This French breed looks similar to the wild mallard but is much bigger – often reaching 12lb. Although its size would suggest it would be good as a table bird, it grows slowly, so it's not popular with commercial breeders. Egg-laying is poor, too. *(continued)*

Silver appleyard

A great dual-purpose breed – a good layer and an excellent table bird – and it looks good too, with a mallard-like green head and silvery-grey and fawn feathers elsewhere. There is a miniature version of the breed, too.

The Welsh breeds

Yes, there are some! The Welsh harlequin is a popular bird, similar in plumage to the silver appleyard, but smaller. It's another descendant of the khaki campbell, but has a much calmer temperament. Excellent layers, and fine for meat if you want a smallish bird. The magpie duck was created in Wales around about 1918 and, as its name suggests, has striking black and white markings, though there is also a blue-grey and white variety. A good size for the table, it lays blue-green eggs.

Ducklings or adult ducks?

It's easy to be tempted by ducklings – we were. They're undeniably cute, they're cheap, and you'll be able to tame them much more easily than older birds. But, as always, there are drawbacks, too. The first thing you need to know is that if you're offered a box of motherless, fluffy ducklings, you'll have to keep them under a brooder lamp (an infra-red light, which is suspended above the birds to keep them warm) until they get their first feathers. Until they are completely feathered, duckings which have been raised artificially shouldn't be allowed access to a pond, because they won't be waterproof. The preen gland, found at the base of the tail, secretes an oil which the bird spreads, using its beak, onto its feathers and claws. In the natural world, a duck will preen her young until they can manage by themselves, giving them the all-important waterproofing. Motherless ducklings, however, have to learn to do it themselves, so the whole process takes longer.

I advised against raising chickens from tiny chicks in the previous section, and I would strongly suggest that your first ducks should be either young adults or fully feathered ducklings. Again, buy from a reputable breeder. Newcomers to ducks won't necessarily know how to tell a duck from a drake, and the advantage of buying from a breeder is that the stock will already have been sexed, and you can specify what you want, so you won't have any unwelcome surprises.

Ducks and water

Ducks need access to water, but you don't *have* to have a pond. Obviously, a pond is a more natural environment, but, unless it's the kind that is fed by a spring, it will be dirty in no time at all. Ducks need to be able to wash and preen, but they can do this in a container like a children's paddling pool or a strong baby bath. The key is to have something deep enough for them to completely submerge their heads in, and heavy enough not to tip over. It will need to be cleaned out and refilled every day, because stagnant water can be dangerous, but it could be the solution if you can't have or don't want a pond.

Accommodation

Ready-made duck houses aren't seen as regularly as chicken houses, but you should be able to find a supplier by checking the specialist smallholder magazines. However, it's easy to modify an existing chicken shed or rabbit house to suit. As a general rule, large breeds of duck should have around 2sq ft (0.19 m^2) each, and the internal height of the house should be about 3ft (90cm). If you're adapting a chicken house, take out the perch (ducks don't roost like hens) and block up the pop-holes, which will be too small for ducks to use to get in and out. Ducks can use the main door for access. The drawback is that you have to shut them in at night and let them out the next day but, if you want a regular supply of eggs, you're going to have to do this in any case. Unfortunately, ducks aren't like hens, returning to their house to lay their eggs. If they are allowed to come and go as they please, they'll start laying all over the place; unless you keep them locked in until they have laid (usually first thing in the morning), every day will be like an Easter egg hunt. We made the mistake of not training our ducks to be herded in at night. The result was that (a) we lost a lot of ducks to foxes until we put up a perimeter fence; and (b) we kept the local corvid population stuffed to the gunnels. Ducks will lay eggs all over the place – even in the pond as they are swimming – so be warned.

Ducks and drakes: how many?

Well, the simple answer is, if you don't want to breed from your ducks, don't bother with a drake. Just as you don't need a cockerel to get your hens to lay eggs, you don't need a drake to get your ducks in the mood, either. Ducks are often sold as trios – one drake and two ducks – but a ratio of one to seven is kinder and more natural. Drakes are really rough and voracious lovers and, in my experience, will spend all day mounting any female in sight. By increasing the size of the harem, the 'workload' is shared more reasonably. Given the choice, though, I wouldn't have a drake again.

Ailments

On the whole, ducks are much healthier creatures than chickens, as long as you remember the key things: sufficient food, clean water and clean surroundings. Lameness is something which occurs from time to time – often just muscle strains caused by getting in and out of the water or the duck house awkwardly. Like chickens, they can also pick up worms – the internal, parasitic sort – from wild birds, but treatments are widely available. One of the most serious conditions affecting waterfowl is botulism, a killer caused by a bacterium found in stagnant water. The secret lies in prevention, of course – keeping ponds and water containers free of dirty water.

Geese

Despite a slight nervousness around geese, I've often been tempted to get some in. There is a growing demand for geese for the table and, every year, when we take our turkey orders, we always get requests for these fine, big birds as an alternative to the more modern festive roast. They are certainly back in fashion – a fact borne out by the phenomenal price per kilo when compared against other meat birds. Research carried out for the rural and environmental consultancy ADAS recently revealed that goose meat is better for us than we might have thought. Studies showed that the meat had a lower fat content than lamb and beef. In addition, the fat contained a relatively low proportion of the 'bad' saturated fats, but a higher proportion of the 'good' mono-unsaturated and essential fatty acids.

I have so far shied away from them because they seem such fussy things. Geese are rather selective eaters, which means they will nibble all your tender young blades of grass, but leave all the older, longer, tougher stuff along with all those weeds you'd like to get rid of. Other birds help keep down grass and weeds and reduce the amount of mowing you'll have to do, but geese can have you working even harder. Because they prefer the new growth, you may have to get the mower out more often, in order to encourage it. Grass also needs to be kept short because coarse older grass can cause crop-binding, which can kill.

Some people I know have got around the problem by keeping the geese alongside other livestock – cattle or sheep will eat the stronger stuff, leaving the new growth for the geese. The birds should thrive on good grass, but some supplementary feeding – chicken pellets mixed with wheat is a popular choice – can be given late afternoon.

The tolerance levels of your neighbours should be a consideration when deciding whether or not to raise geese. Ducks may be noisy, but geese win the contest hands down every time, so make sure that those who live nearest to you are prepared for what you are thinking of inflicting on them. Geese can be pretty nasty creatures, too. I can't forget my first sight of geese as a child. My nan lived in Dowlais Top, on the outskirts of Merthyr Tydfil, and my younger brother and I spent many happy times playing on the slag heaps (well, Nan called them mountains). Thousands of men flocked to the areas from other parts of the UK and abroad to find work in the iron industry – so much so that one area became known as Klondike because of the mad rush to settle there. My childhood memories of Klondike were of tiny terraced cottages hidden behind the busy high street, with back gardens full of vegetables, fruit bushes, flowers and washing lines. The gardens backed onto a stretch of rough land where the householders would let their chickens, ducks and – worst of all – their geese roam free.

Nan's idea of a good day out was to take us walking there to look for goose feathers, which she would dye with pink food colouring and make into feather dusters. The downside was that the geese were a fierce, hissing bunch, frighteningly territorial, and always ready to give chase. Sometimes we would get away with it, taking home a shopping bag full of lovely strong, white feathers, but most of the time our afternoon stroll would turn into a 200-yard sprint back to the safety of the high street.

Goose-lovers have since assured me that not all geese are aggressive, particularly if they are well socialized when young, but I remain unconvinced about the merits of keeping them. Old memories die hard.

One word of warning if you have young children with small pets: geese are omnivores and will eat anything from slugs, snails and worms to mice, baby rats and even hamsters, so don't leave them unsupervised unless you fancy another trip to the pet shop!

Choosing breeds

Your choice of bird will be largely determined by the reason for keeping geese – whether for meat, eggs or as pets. Good laying birds will produce about 60 eggs a year – with each egg the equivalent in size to about three hen eggs. Geese fall into three groups – light (4.5–8kg/10–18lb), medium (6.5–9kg/14–20lbs) and heavy (9–16kg/20–35lb). Ganders are naturally heavier in all breeds. Some of the most popular – but by no means the only – breeds are shown in the box.

Light geese

Chinese

Be warned, these are regarded as the noisiest and most aggressive of all breeds, and are often chosen by people who want birds which will raise the alarm at the first sign of intruders. Descended from the wild swan goose, there are two colour types, white and brown. Chinese geese have a prominent 'knob' above the bill, similar to swans.

Pilgrim

If Chinese geese are the rogues of the species, Pilgrims are the angels, much prized for their gentle temperament. Originally from Britain, the bird was taken to the USA by the Pilgrim Fathers. The goslings can be sexed on hatching, because of the colour of the down and bill. Adult males are mainly white with some grey; females are light grey, with white feathers at the front of the head.

Roman

Imported to other parts of Europe at the turn of the nineteenth century, these are short, stocky, mainly white birds which are easily recognized by their short necks and small body length. Popular as a meat bird and a good breeder.

Sebastopol

The origins of the Sebastopol is unclear, though the name suggests it came from the Crimea. Most birds are white, but a buff variety also exists. Interestingly, there are two variations in plumage: the frizzle, which has curly feathers all over the body, but not on the head and neck, and the smooth-breasted. *(continued)*

Medium geese

Brecon buff

Let's start with a good Welsh breed, very popular for meat, eggs and showing. Buff and white plumage, with a pink beak and feet. Hardy and used to the wet Welsh climate, it needs access to water more than some breeds, and also prefers to forage rather than be kept in a yard. Considered a fairly placid breed, and it doesn't fly a lot. Good for beginners.

Pomeranian

A German breed descended from the European Greylag, colours include grey and white saddleback. Broad-chested, after decades of careful breeding for meat, a distinctive bold head and an orange-pink bill. The heavy breast means the birds look horizontal rather than upright.

West of England

This – along with the Pilgrim – is thought to be the original or 'common goose' of Britain during Victorian times. Goslings are sex-linked for colour, the female being grey or a mixture of grey and white, and the male plain white.

Heavy Geese

African

A large, striking bird with a prominent 'knob' above the beak and a smooth, semi-circular gullet or dewlap. Plumage is shades of brown, and there is a distinctive brown stripe running from the top of the head down to the base of the neck. Very loud and in-your-face, they might be a bit daunting for a beginner.

American buff

Plumage is fawn with a paler abdomen; brown eyes and orange feet and bill. Developed in the US after fifty years of selective breeding from the general farm goose. Characterized by orange-buff feathers, with markings similar to the Toulouse. Very docile and good parents.

Embden

One of the most popular table birds. The tallest of all the breeds, often standing more than 1m high, with an extremely long body and neck. Plumage is plain white. Females can weigh 28lb (12.5kg), males up to 34lb (15.5kg).

Toulouse

Like the Embden, this is another bird which was specially bred as a meat bird, particularly for use by producers of *paté de fois gras*. Because of their large size, they can have trouble moving around and – not surprisingly – mating. Need to be kept on fairly flat ground. Gentle birds, good as pets. Normally grey, but occasionally in white and buff. The bill is orange-red and the feet are flesh-coloured.

Rearing geese

Many breeds are excellent grazers, and professional producers say an acre of land can accommodate as many as forty birds. Personally, I'd halve that number, but that's purely because I believe in giving all birds plenty of space to roam around. It also reduces the risk of bullying, which can be a problem when stocking densities are high, and lessens problems with parasites.

Geese can be used to weed a variety of crops and to keep fence rows, ditches and inaccessible areas clean. They are also effective in controlling pond weeds. Raising geese in orchards may be a simple method of controlling grass growth. Remember, however, that pesticides and slug pellets are toxic to geese.

Commercial breeders tend to house their birds in pole barns or open sheds; geese don't need fancy housing, just shelter from sun and heavy rain, and protection at night from predators, of course. A normal garden shed can easily be adapted by replacing glass windows with wire netting for ventilation.

Geese make a mess of their sleeping quarters, so a thin layer of wood shavings or sawdust will help keep the floor dry and soak up droppings. Some people prefer houses with slatted floors. The gaps between the slats need to be wide enough to allow droppings to pass through. Bear in mind that eventually, as muck builds up under the slats, you will have to resite the house.

Your shed should ideally have nest boxes, which can be purpose-built or made out of the kind of wooden crates you find in the grocer's shop. You don't really need a pond. Access to clean water is sufficient, but geese love having access to water – they will be cleaner, and some people say they mate more readily.

Turkeys

I began raising turkeys for the first time about six years ago and I've never looked back. Many livestock keepers believe turkeys are difficult to rear, and this puts them off having a go themselves. Now it's probably not in my financial interest to burst the bubble of mystique surrounding turkeys, but I'll do it, all the same. Rearing turkeys is not rocket science. Yes, they're more unpredictable than other birds, and they need a lot more attention when they're small, but it all comes down to common sense and good husbandry.

My first turkeys were an impulse buy at auction. They were bog-standard commercial birds – white-feathered and bred to grow fast – and I got them at five weeks old. Looking back, the trio were quite hard work, because they insisted on roosting on top of the shed at night – if you've ever tried stretching on tip-toes to try and wrench a stubborn, 20lb turkey off a 6ft-high shed in the snow, you'll understand what I mean. I've since learned the benefits of clipping the flight feathers.

Apart from refusing to use any form of shelter (they preferred to sit outside, even when it was snowing heavily), they were otherwise enjoyable to rear. It's hard not to find them appealing – and very difficult not to get attached to them. Eating the first one was difficult, but by the time I was taking fifty identical birds to the abattoir, personalities didn't come into it.

Choosing your turkeys

Even though my first turkeys were from a commercial strain, bred to turn food into meat as quickly as possible, it must be said that they tasted amazing. There is just no comparison between shed-raised and free-range turkeys, and the same is true of all other birds. The old adage, 'You are what you eat' is true, but it must also be said that where, when and how the birds eat is equally as important. My birds feed when they want to, exercise as they like and roost in the same way as they would in the wild. Their lives are short, but good. When I got my first turkeys, a builder who was working for us at the time said: 'You want to lock them up in a shed so they can't run around. That's the way to put weight on them.' Needless to say, I didn't think much of his advice and I certainly didn't follow it.

Choosing breeds

Turkey breed names normally refer to their plumage, for example, Norfolk black, bronze, white, buff, bourbon red and blue or slate – though the Cröllwitzer, which is a striking white bird with black banding, is a bit of an exception. Generally, if you're looking for turkeys to rear for meat, you're only going to be offered black, bronze or white; these are the only types reared on a commercial scale here in the UK, and the white is still the most popular.

The author has been raising traditional bronze turkeys for several years.

We've already established that free-range commercial turkeys are streets ahead of indoor-reared ones, but there is also a world of difference between the meat of white turkeys and that of the more traditional varieties. Demand for bronze turkeys – the kind I raise every year – has grown steadily over the past few years, thanks to top chefs like Gordon Ramsay praising them for their superior flavour. Until the 1950s, most turkeys were bronze or black, with only the occasional white 'mutant'. Eventually, fashion changed and demand grew for fast-growing white birds which were cheaper to produce and looked neater when plucked (no matter how meticulous you are, dark feathers leave dark quills in the skin). Thankfully, taste is once again triumphing over presentation.

Bronze turkeys are more closely related to the original wild turkeys, and consequently are slower growing and reach smaller weights. You can order light or heavy strains, but they only vary by a few pounds. My birds typically reach between 12lb (5.4kg) and 15lb (6.8kg) – ample for most families. One of the most grotesque sights I've ever seen is a lorry load of overweight white turkeys, destined for the catering trade, being dropped off at the abattoir. Barn-raised and fed to bursting point, they were too big to walk and, judging by the soiled feathers, hadn't done so for some time. Such is the price that must be paid for cheap meat.

Starting with turkeys

If you're unsure about raising turkeys for the first time, you'll be best off buying in growers – young birds about six weeks old which are fully feathered and therefore don't need too much mollycoddling. It's cheaper – and, in some ways, more satisfying – to raise them from day-old poults, but much more challenging and time-consuming.

You'll have to order your birds well in advance (check the classified ads in specialist magazines for dealers who will deliver), because there aren't that many breeders who will supply small numbers. I generally place my order about May, and get the birds delivered in mid-July or early August – no later, otherwise they won't reach the right weight by Christmas. A free-range bronze turkey needs about twenty-two weeks to grow to table weight, but white ones will grow faster.

I always buy hens, rather than a mixture of hens and stags. It's slightly more expensive, but it means there is less chance of fighting in the ranks. Stags will, of course, give you larger birds, but my customers don't like giant-size turkeys.

The poults are delivered to me straight from the hatchery, and they go into a secure shed with a floor covered in wood shavings and heated by overhead infra-red brooder lamps, which are turned on an hour or so before their arrival. I started off using purpose-built brooder cages, which are great for new arrivals, but turkey poults grow at an amazing rate, and quickly get too big for their surroundings. Now we use a wooden partition to divide a shed into two areas – one for the birds and lamps and the other for storing the feed.

Tiny poults need a tremendous amount of heat – after all, just imagine how warm it must be under a fully grown turkey. The temperature needs to stay around 35°C for the first two weeks of their lives, gradually decreasing as they get older, but you have to

These 4-week-old turkey poults are now ready to explore the great outdoors.

watch their behaviour and adjust the height of the brooder lamps accordingly; too warm and you will see the birds gasping; too cold and they will huddle together for warmth, often smothering one another in the process.

Many people who decide to raise poultry get themselves a good book and then terrify themselves by reading the section on the illnesses. With turkey poults, the biggest cause of death in the early weeks is not sickness, but smothering. All tiny birds huddle together for warmth and, as they clamber on top of one another, someone has to end up at the bottom of the pile. Drowning is also a danger, so make sure you have purpose-made chick drinkers – the balloon-shaped kind which you invert, fill with water, screw onto the base, and then stand the right way up. These let just enough water out into the 'moat' in the base – too shallow for poults to drown in.

Some people I know reckon that turkey poults tend to die of fright. I've not had any experience of this, but I do take one precaution which some more seasoned poultry-rearers may consider a little barking mad: I let them listen to the radio. Years ago, someone who incubated rare breed chickens, hundreds at a time, said he found that leaving a radio on in the brooding shed got the chicks used to strange and sudden noises, with the result that when he entered the shed, he didn't send the whole lot flying in different directions in a mad panic. I tried it with the chicks I bought from him and it seemed to work, so I've done it with turkey poults ever since. They listen to Radio Four every day.

Potential problems

Early deaths put a lot of people off rearing turkeys. It's not nice going down to the shed in the morning, only to have to pick up another tiny dead body. Generally, though, if your poults don't die in the first four weeks, they stand a good chance of survival. We always expect to lose at least 10 per cent in the first month, either through general, unexplained 'fading' or suffocation from huddling.

Once they're fully feathered and out to grass, you have little to worry about – apart from the mysterious killer called blackhead. Birds lose interest in food, droppings turn yellow and runny, and there is often a darkening of the skin and wattles on the head – hence the name 'blackhead' – before they eventually die. Blackhead – histomoniasis, to give it its proper name – is a disease which attacks the digestive tract of turkeys. Chickens can carry the disease without being affected by it, and it can lie dormant in the soil for years. The usual advice given is never to keep chickens and turkeys together. However, for people with restricted space that just isn't practical. The key rule I've always followed is to make sure you worm your hens regularly, as *Heterakis gallinae* (the caecal roundworm) is the little varmint which is to blame for the problem. Wild birds can also carry the worm, of course, so it pays to feed and water your turkeys indoors if at all possible.

Turkeys, once fully grown, are pretty hardy creatures, and can withstand severe extremes of weather. Every year, I find myself brushing snow off the backs of ours, because they just don't seem to see the merit of sheltering in a blizzard. Strange birds. They don't do well in wet weather, however, and you might have a battle on your hands trying to get them to shelter. They may still stubbornly want to stay outdoors, but they are more prone to ailments in wet weather, so try and get them indoors if you possibly can.

Hatching your own

Whenever I write about turkeys in my *Western Mail* column, I always get e-mails and letters from readers keen to have a go at rearing their own. The best advice I can give is to buy from a reputable breeder and get yourself some authoritative books on poultry-keeping (see the recommended reading list at the end of this section). I had an e-mail recently asking where turkey eggs could be bought, as the writer wanted to try hatching his own. Personally, I wouldn't bother. You have to find someone prepared to sell you some eggs and, as there aren't that many people rearing turkeys in huge numbers in Wales, I think tracking some down is going to be a tall order. Last year, I saw a few batches of turkey eggs being sold on eBay, and I was amazed to see half a dozen going for £30 or more, on a regular basis. Part of the problem is that turkeys just don't lay as many eggs as hens. Your average chicken lays about 250 eggs a year, but turkeys are more likely to manage about 100 during the breeding season – a season which lasts just five months. If you're intent on hatching your own, it might be worth contacting one of the big poultry producers, like Cyril Bason in Shropshire (01588 673204 or e-mail *cyril-bason@cyril-bason.co.uk*), or contacting the Turkey Club UK (01223 262484 or see the website *www.turkeyclub.org.uk*).

Feeding

Unfortunately, turkeys can't be treated like other poultry when it comes to feeding. They don't thrive well enough on rations designed for chickens when they are very young, though these feeds can be used in an emergency. Talk to your local feed merchant well in advance of getting your poults, as not all outlets consider it worthwhile stocking turkey feed on the off-chance of a customer calling by. Depending on how many birds you plan to rear, it might pay to have a bulk order delivered direct from the manufacturers – but bear in mind that, to qualify for a discount, you'll normally have to order a minimum of a tonne. This takes up quite a bit of space, and you'll have to keep it dry and also safe from nibbling rodents.

Like all young birds, turkey poults need to be started off on high-protein crumbs – but these should be specifically designed for turkeys, containing between 24 per cent and 28 per cent protein. I feed the starter crumbs until about 6 weeks (though some people suggest keeping them on crumbs until they're 8 weeks old) and then gradually get them onto a grower ration in pellet form. I do this by mixing crumbs and pellets together, so they slowly get used to the new texture. Later, I start introducing mixed corn, plus any spare fruit and vegetables.

If you listen to the textbooks, turkey poults are notoriously difficult to start eating and drinking. I've not found any problems myself, but what I have noticed is that they don't like eating off the floor. They don't have the natural habit of scratching around like chickens, so any spilled food just stays there and is wasted – particularly annoying as turkey food usually costs £2 or £3 more per bag than layers' pellets. Get yourself some spill-resistant feeders, and also make sure that whatever containers you use (you can get purpose-made chick feeders) are big enough for all the poults to feed at the same time, so they're not jockeying for position.

One of the great pleasures of rearing turkeys is seeing their reaction to new foods. I give them as varied a selection as possible – anything spare from the vegetable garden and the greenhouse, or anything I can find reduced at the supermarket. Depending on what's available, they can be feasting on anything from peppers and pumpkins to broccoli and broad beans. Turkeys can see colours, so it's good to give them a bright array of treats from time to time to help relieve the boredom.

Two weeks before slaughter, my birds go onto a finisher ration or a standard chicken feed – layers' pellets mixed with corn, and I gradually increase the corn and vegetables. The morning before they go to the abattoir, they get a final feed – a kind of Last Supper – and from then on, they'll just have water.

Accommodation

Living accommodation for turkeys is simple. A pole barn – a three-sided structure, open to the elements on one side – is all that most turkeys require. As I mentioned earlier, turkeys don't seem to feel the cold the way we do, so don't be surprised if your best efforts are ignored. If the weather really does turn bad, or if avian flu strikes, you might have to force your birds indoors, however, so plan how you might do it.

Once our turkeys are outdoors, their home is a temporary but secure paddock made of fence posts and 2 inch-square Weldmesh fencing cable-tied to the posts. This, in turn, is bordered by an electric fence to deter foxes. We pull our livestock trailer into the enclosure, fill it with straw, fit a few perches, and leave it with the door open. The great benefit of using the trailer is that, when it reaches time to go to the abattoir, we just have to herd the birds in and close the door. Then it's just a case of dropping the electric fence and snipping a few of the cable ties attaching the metal fence to the wooden posts, and driving out.

Other birds

Once you've got the poultry-keeping bug, chances are you'll end up with all sorts of things. Visiting poultry auctions opens up a whole new world of possibilities, from tiny quail and noisy guinea fowl to other gourmet favourites like pheasants and partridges. When you've mastered the basics of brooding young birds, there will be no stopping you. The great thing is that nothing need be a rare and expensive delicacy any longer when you can rear it yourself. All you need to do is get yourself some good books, take advice from breeders wherever possible and apply the same high standard of husbandry that you give the birds you already have.

One word of warning, however: if you're thinking about keeping ornamental birds, try to steer away from peacocks. They often appear in livestock auctions, but everyone I know who has been tempted to buy some has had bitter regrets. They may look beautiful but, as anyone who has lived in close proximity to some will know, they are incredibly noisy with their piercing calls, and they can devastate a well-stocked flower border or vegetable patch in no time at all. They can also do serious damage to relations with your neighbours. Paignton Zoo was forced to destroy some of its wandering flock in June 2007 following complaints from nearby residents, and similar neighbourhood disputes have erupted across the UK.

RECOMMENDED BOOKS

Chris and Mike Ashton, *The Domestic Duck,* Crowood Press, 2001

Tom Bartlett, *Ducks and Geese – A Guide to Management,* Crowood Press, 1988

David Bland, *Turkeys: A Guide to Management,* Crowood Press, 2000

Len Chappel, *Modern Pheasant Rearing,* Gold Cockerel Series, 2006

Chris Graham, *Choosing and Keeping Chickens,* Hamlyn, 2006

Martin Gurdon, *Hen and the Art of Chicken Maintenance,* New Holland, 2003

Dave Holderread, *Storey's Guide to Raising Ducks,* Storey Books, 2000

Janice Houghton-Wallace, *Not Just for Christmas – The Complete Guide to Raising Turkeys,* Farming Books & Videos, 2007

Humane Slaughter Association, *Practical Slaughter of Poultry: A Guide for the Small Producer, www.hsa.org.uk* or tel. 01582 831919

G. T. Klein, *Starting Right with Turkeys,* Storey Books, 2005

Charlotte Popescu, *Best Hens For You,* Cavalier Paperbacks, 2006

David Sainsbury, *Poultry Health and Management: Chickens, Ducks, Turkeys, Geese, Quail,* WileyBlackwell, 1999

Katie Thear, *Free-Range Poultry,* Whittet Books, 2002

—— *Incubation: A Guide to Hatching and Rearing,* Broad Leys Publishing, 1997

—— *Keeping Quail: A Guide to Domestic and Commercial Management,* Broad Leys Publishing, 2005

—— *Starting with Chickens,* Broad Leys Publishing, 1999

—— *Starting with Ducks,* Broad Leys Publishing, 2002

—— *Starting with Geese,* Broad Leys Publishing, 2003

—— *Starting with Turkeys,* Broad Leys Publishing, 2006

Carol Twinch, *Poultry: A Guide to Management,* Crowood Press, 1985
John Walters and Michael Parker, *Keeping Ducks, Geese and Turkeys,* Pelham Books, 1976

MAGAZINES

Practical Poultry (*www.practicalpoultry.co.uk*), published monthly
Country Smallholding (*www.countrysmallholding.com*), published monthly with a dedicated
    poultry section

WEBSITES

www.backyardchickens.com Backyard Chickens
www.basc.org.uk British Association for Shooting and Conservation
www.domestic-waterfowl.co.uk The Domestic Waterfowl Club of Great Britain
www.feathersite.com Feathersite
www.gooseclub.org.uk The Goose Club
www.howtoraisequail.com How to Raise Quail
www.pheasant.org.uk The World Pheasant Association
www.poultry.uk.com British Poultry Council
www.poultryclub.org Poultry Club of Great Britain
www.poultrypages.com
www.quailsfromwales.org.uk Quails from Wales
www.quailtalk.com Game Bird and Conservation Gazette
www.thepoultrysite.com The Poultry Site
www.turkeyclub.org.uk The Turkey Club of Great Britain
www.waterfowl.org.uk British Waterfowl Association

Four-Legged Livestock

Now that you're moving on to 'proper' animals, you'll start discovering the real bureau-
cracy surrounding farming. It's all there for a good reason, of course, but you won't find
anyone saying they enjoy filling in forms and keeping records. Your first step is to get
your holding registered, and flock/herd numbers for any sheep, goats, cattle, or pigs (see
Chapter 7). You'll have to start dealing with various Welsh Assembly Government
departments and your local trading standards department, which handles animal
movement documentation and will issue you with forms which have to be completed
every time stock (cattle excepted – again, see Chapter 7) are moved.

Even more importantly, you're shifting up a whole gear in livestock terms. Most of
the time, rearing animals with feathers is a fairly easy business, requiring little in the way
of veterinary expertise. Sheep, goats, pigs, cattle – or anything else you choose to rear –
need a great deal of routine 'maintenance', requiring a whole new set of skills, so seek
out some training before you make a decision to take on something you might not be
able to handle. Get yourself on some training courses (see Chapter 5) and visit some

neighbouring farmers so you can see for yourself the kind of duties you'll be expected to perform – everyday things like giving injections and oral medicines, caring for feet and treating minor injuries.

You should, of course, find a good farm vet as soon as you get your livestock. Where I live, vets who treat livestock are disappearing fast, even though small animal veterinary surgeries are springing up all over the place. Get your vet to call on you even before you need help – simply to check over your livestock and make sure everything is fine. The vet will be happy to show you how to administer drugs and explain, for instance, the sites for different types of injections.

You will probably feel happier calling out the vet for routine jobs the first couple of times – and you should always do so if you don't feel sufficiently confident. However, by the time subsequent treatments are needed, you may be ready to do the job yourself, which means getting hold of drugs from your vet. Most vets will not give out certain drugs unless they have visited your stock recently (at least in the past year).

Communicable diseases
I can't start this section of the book without mentioning the kind of words which send shudders through all farmers. Diseases like foot-and-mouth, BSE, bluetongue, bovine tuberculosis (bTB) and anthrax have rarely been out of the news in recent years. Thankfully, the organizations with responsibility for dealing with such outbreaks – the Welsh Assembly Government in Wales and DEFRA in England – learned some serious lessons following the disastrous foot-and-mouth outbreak of 2001.

There has been widespread criticism that restrictions put in place during the 2007 outbreaks were far too stringent, but in fairness to the authorities it must be a difficult call to make when the safety of the bulk of the UK's livestock is potentially at risk. Keeping farmers up to date with the latest information regarding animal movement restrictions is vitally important, and one innovative development in 2007 was the introduction of a system of sending updates as voice messages to mobile phones.

But what can we, as farmers, do to protect our animals? Vaccination may be appropriate in some circumstances, of course, but everything comes back to good husbandry – keeping a close eye on your stock for changes in behaviour or appearance, checking for tell-tale signs on a regular basis, and, of course, observing high standards of biosecurity, both on our own farms and when visiting others.

Sheep

For some bizarre reason, newcomers to smallholding seem to assume that sheep are easy to keep. It's amazing how many people I've heard saying things like: 'Oh, we're going to throw a couple of sheep in the field to keep the grass down and give us some lamb for the freezer.' Sounds so straightforward, doesn't it? Yet sheep are deceptive creatures: people see them roaming the hills in all weathers and seem to assume they look after themselves. Here's the news: THEY DON'T!

It took me quite a few years before I plucked up the courage to keep sheep. First came the poultry, then the goats. I started off buying in two ewes, each with twin lambs already at foot. That was the easy bit. My first medical challenge was dealing with mastitis – an uncomfortable inflammation of the udder which can kill if not treated. Sod's law, it had to be the wildest of the two – Ugly Betty, a manic Welsh Mountain who panics at the blink of an eyelid. It took three of us to get her into the trailer for the vet to inspect her, and she really wasn't happy about it. The vet left me with some syringes and antibiotics and instructions to give her a shot every day for five days. Luckily, I'd had some experience of injecting thanks to the smallholder course I did a few years earlier, but I was still nervous. My patient wasn't at all impressed, but I did it, and it got easier every time.

Last spring was the worst time I've ever had since becoming a smallholder. It was my first 'solo' lambing season. I had delivered lambs on the smallholders' course at the agricultural college, under the watchful eye of my tutor, and again on refresher courses, but I had never done it unsupervised. The first ewe to show signs of lambing was Ugly Betty. Just my luck. Her labour seemed to be going on and on so, after looking through all my books and ringing up Phil, my old tutor, for moral support, I had to intervene. First, of course, we had to catch her – again, a team effort involving three of us. I realized then

Buying in ewes with lambs is one way of starting off your flock.

that I had missed an important and very practical step leading up to lambing – getting the mothers-to-be indoors and into lambing pens well before their due dates. It not only helps you ensure the ewes get the nutrition they need, but also means you've got them in a controlled environment, should there be any problems. Much better than running up and down a steep hill as it's starting to get dark!

Fortunately, I managed to deliver two lovely big healthy ewe lambs – a fantastically satisfying experience, but something you really shouldn't attempt without training. I was so glad I had already had the chance to deliver two under supervision, in the safety of a 'classroom' situation in the college barn, before having to attempt it on my own.

The other drama that occurred during my first lambing season was a vaginal prolapse. Now that really was scary. I thought that the Suffolk cross was starting to give birth when I saw something emerging from her rear end but – horror of horrors – it was the vagina! What happens is that the vagina turns inside out and emerges like a big red, fleshy football. It can be pushed back in – but with a lot of effort, because it's huge by comparison to the orifice you're trying to squeeze it through, and it keeps on wanting to pop back out. If it does decide to go back in, it has to be held in place with something – most commonly a prolapse 'spoon' – but there is always the risk of it coming out again. The other danger after a prolapse is that the ewe can get blood poisoning. Despite injecting mine with antibiotics, as instructed by the vet, she died a few days later, along with the twins she was carrying.

As if all that wasn't enough, the final sheep-related disaster of the year was a bout of fly-strike (see Chapter 12). Flies lay their eggs in the fleece and when the maggots hatch out, they work their way in and begin devouring the flesh. It's probably one of the most disgusting things you will ever see – certainly top of my list, and I've seen some pretty horrible sights in my time. I noticed the ewe – unlucky old Dotty, who had had a stillborn lamb just a few weeks earlier – was scratching herself. Fortunately, I caught it in time, got a friend to whip off the fleece and treat the area quickly, and she lived to tell the tale. From then on, I made a resolution to shear as early as possible.

So, are you really prepared?

Not been put off yet? Well done. As you've seen from my own experiences, sheep can be pretty high-maintenance creatures. Problems associated with lambing are pretty scary, and I'm not going to go into detail about them in this book, because I really believe you should get to know sheep before even contemplating breeding.

However, even if you exclude pregnancy and birthing difficulties, sheep are fairly demanding. For a start, their feet will always need regular trimming, they'll need worming, and there are a whole host of other ailments, diseases (aside from the newsworthy ones like foot-and-mouth and bluetongue), and assorted health problems which will need taking care of. You'll need to learn how to administer drugs – both orally and by injection. Are you sure you want to do all this? Can you cope? And will anyone help if you need assistance?

Shearing is essential to protect sheep from fly-strike.

Why not just keep it simple?

If you've decided that you really do want sheep, the next decision is what you want them for and at what age to buy them. Some people just like the idea of sheep on their land. I read somewhere that estate agents reckon the sight of an attractive flock of sheep grazing happily could add as much as £10,000 to the price of a house. Hard to imagine? It's all about buying the dream, apparently. House-hunters are mugs when faced with a pretty view.

If all you want are lawnmowers which look nice in the fields in front of the house, why not think about getting someone else's sheep in for occasional grazing? It's the most hassle-free way of keeping sheep, with none of the responsibility (apart from making sure your boundary fences are secure and keeping an eye on the flock to ensure there aren't any welfare problems you should tell the owner about). For generations, hill farmers have sent sheep away 'on tack' to lower-lying holdings to avoid the worst of the winter weather, taking them away again once the spring grass has started to sprout well back home.

However, if you really want a flock of your own, there are some other alternatives which will allow you to savour the excitement of being a sheep farmer whilst, at the same time, avoiding all that messy birthing business and other nasty jobs like the tricky business of castration. If your aim is to raise meat for the table, or to sell on to others, it's worth thinking about buying in ready-weaned lambs for a limited amount of time. One option is buying ewe lambs in the autumn which can then be sold on as what are known as shearling ewes the next year. These will be bought as ewes to breed from. Another alternative is buying in lambs to fatten for slaughter. This can be done quickly or slowly, depending on your circumstances, needs, and preferences. Some farmers buy in lambs towards the end of July or beginning of August and aim to finish them (i.e. get them to the required weight) in less than three months. Other people prefer to let their lambs grow at a slower rate. There are some benefits to be had by buying in lambs when there are lots of them flooding the market in about October or November, and rearing them for the early spring market – before the 'new season' lamb is ready. The drawback of this is that your grass won't be at its best through the winter months, so you will have to feed some kind of supplement to make sure they get the nutrition they need.

When it comes to determining whether a lamb is ready for slaughter, you need to 'condition score' the animal, which involves placing your hand over the backbone in the area just behind the rib cage. Ask a friendly farmer or your vet to show you how it is done. There is a scale of one to five: one is extremely thin, and five is very fat. Three – right in the middle of the scale – is just right. Ewes are often scored several times during the year – the most important time being five to six weeks prior to lambing. This is a crucial time for the growth of the unborn lamb, and feeding should be adjusted according to the ewe's condition.

Orphaned lambs – be warned!

We've all seen pictures of tiny little orphan lambs being bottle-reared – images which really tear at the heartstrings and bring out the nurturing instinct in us all. You'll often find that farmers are only too glad to give away orphaned lambs – simply because bottle-feeding them several times a day and keeping them warm under an infra-red lamp is too much like hard work when you've maybe hundreds or thousands of ewes lambing and a busy farm business to run. They may even need the technique called tubing – feeding by inserting a tube down into the stomach (or the lungs, if you slip up and get it badly wrong!) if they aren't keen to take milk from a bottle. Having bottle-reared four puppies (feeding every two hours, night and day) not so long ago, I know how time-consuming it can be, taking on the role of surrogate mother. Lambs are no easier; if anything, they require more attention.

How and what to buy

I know I keep saying it, but buy from a reputable breeder. Ask your farming neighbours for recommendations or contact the relevant breed society if you have a particular breed in mind (see below). As with all animals, it's best to choose a breed that is well-suited to the conditions on offer, so again, ask locally for advice.

Follow the basic rules for buying an animal in good health, outlined near the beginning of this chapter – watch for sickly appearance and poor posture; discharge from eyes or nose; scouring (diarrhoea); poor coat/skin and scratching; coughing or sneezing; lameness or other signs of pain or discomfort. When choosing both sheep and goats, feet and teeth require particular scrutiny. Buy a sheep with badly overgrown or misshapen feet and you're asking for trouble, so take someone with you who knows what to look out for. Get them to look over the udders at the same time, checking for lumps or problems with the teats.

Choosing breeds

Your best bet is to go for the kind of sheep your experienced farming neighbours have. Chances are, they've been keeping them for generations because they suit the climate and terrain. More often than not, they will be cross-bred – their parents will have been chosen for specific reasons. A big texel or Suffolk ram might be mated with another breed to produce a meatier carcass, for instance. A breed with a smaller head and shoulders may be used if the aim is to produce lambs which are easier to deliver.

Having said all this, you may have long-term plans to build up a pedigree flock. As with most things, personal preferences differ hugely, and what I might think is a handsome sheep (Herdwicks are my favourite), you might not give a second glance. There are so many breeds to choose from, you'll be spoiled for choice, but you should do your research and consider which breeds will do best in your area, and get in touch with breed societies.

Bear in mind that, if you opt for a breed which isn't already reared in your area and you have plans to breed from your sheep, getting access to fresh bloodlines might be a problem. If you only have a small flock, you will constantly be on the lookout for unrelated rams, and so you could find yourself trekking hundreds of miles to find one.

Balwen sheep are small and are said to be easy lambers.

In this section, I've chosen just a handful of the breeds available, so refer to the books and websites I've suggested at the end of this section to find out more.

Badger face Welsh mountain

A good one to start with, as it is not just a native breed, but a smallish one, very hardy, and fairly easy to handle. There are two types of badger face – torddu and torwen. Torddu means 'black belly' and the fleece can be white, grey or light brown, always with distinctive black markings. There are black stripes above the eyes and a wide black stripe running from under the chin, under the belly and right to the end of the tail. The legs are black with a tan stripe. The torwen ('white belly') are almost like a negative of the torddu, with reverse colouring and a smaller eye stripe.

Balwen Welsh mountain

Another excellent, manageable and hardy breed, this one of the original Welsh sheep. The breed came from the Tywi Valley in Carmarthenshire and was almost wiped out in the 1940s by a disastrous winter, which left just one ram. Still classed as a rare breed, it is popular with smallholders. Predominantly black, dark brown or dark grey, it has a white stripe running from the top of the head to the top of the nose – hence the name 'balwen' ('white blaze'). The feet are white and there is white on the tail. Breeders say they have excellent feet, are easy lambers and don't need much supplementary feeding.

Beulah speckled face

Another hardy breed and fairly low-maintenance, this breed has been farmed on the hills of Eppynt, Llanafan, Abergwesyn and Llanwrtyd Wells for more than a century. The white fleece – not surprisingly – is speckled, and the face black with white markings. The Welsh hill speckled face is an attractive derivative – white with black markings on nose, eyes, ears, knees and feet. The breed originated in the Devil's Bridge and hill areas of mid-Wales. It is larger than the Welsh mountain.

Black Welsh mountain

A handsome sheep with a fleece which is thick and easy to handle and doesn't need to be dyed. The breed carries a dominant black gene, so even when cross-bred the offspring is black. They are hardy and undemanding and do not normally need supplementary feeding, being content to eat short, rough grasses.

Brecknock Hill Cheviot

Bred from Cheviot sheep introduced to Breconshire in the mid-nineteenth century, this sheep has a white fleece, face and legs, a thick ruff of wool behind the erect ears and a strong, broad back.   *(continued)*

Hill Radnor

The Hill Radnor is a heavy, hardy breed found mainly in Powys. It has tan-coloured face and legs, which are free from wool, and small, alert ears. The dense fleece is popular with hand-spinners and weavers. The ewes are good mothers, and the breed is good for crossing with other breeds.

Llanwenog

A medium-sized shortwool breed with black legs and head, it has a tuft of wool on the fore-head. Its high-quality wool is sought after by spinners; it is considered docile and easy to manage, and has a reputation for producing plenty of twins. This breed developed in the Teifi Valley area of west Wales in the late nineteenth century from the mixture of several breeds from Wales and the Welsh Borders, including the now extinct Llanllwni.

Lleyn

A hardy, medium-sized breed, this gets its name from the peninsula on Anglesey, where it originated. Easy and prolific lambers, the ewes are good mothers. The wool is white and dense and of good quality and the body is wide-breasted with a long back.

Welsh mountain (hill flock)

Probably a bit too much of a challenge for the complete beginner, the Welsh Mountain is a nervous, flighty sheep – but, nevertheless, a reliable breed well-conditioned to withstand all kinds of harsh weather. It has a white or tan face, it has a strong, dense fleece. There are north and south Wales varieties. The south Wales Mountain is bigger and usually has tan markings on the face and legs, as well as a brown collar. There are two recognized types, the Nelson and the Glamorgan.

Shearing

If you have four or more adult sheep, the Wool Marketing Scheme requires you to register with the BWMB to market your fleece wool. Registration forms are available on application to the Producer Registration and Payments Department of the BWMB. You will be sent an explanation of the marketing system and details of the wool depot authorized to handle your wool. Don't get excited, though – fleeces are worth pennies rather than pounds, and payment depends on quality.

Shearing has to be done, so get yourself trained up, or find someone who will do it for you. I went on an excellent, two-day course organized by the British Wool Marketing Board (see *www.britishwool.org.uk* or tel. 01686 626 811 for details). I have to be honest, though, it nearly killed me. My arms ached, my shoulders ached, my thighs ached, and my bottom ached. I was black and blue with nasty bruises and covered in scratches. Oh, and I smelled terrible – even after bathing every day for almost a week. I was left with that feeling you get when you suddenly decide to go back to the gym after you've missed a couple of weeks; that feeling when your body rebels and all your muscles scream 'Please – no more!'

And the best bit was, I only did one day of the two-day course. Unfortunately (or was it a blessing in disguise?) I got a call which meant I had to work on the second day. Just as well, really, because I think another 9 a.m.–5 p.m. session of sheep wrestling would have finished me. What I hadn't counted on was just how physically demanding the day would be. Turning a sheep over for a few minutes to trim its feet can be a bit of an effort, but not too bad at all. But gripping each kicking, wriggling sheep between your knees for 10 minutes or more while you simultaneously shuffle around it with a potentially lethal electrical weapon requires rather more strength and a great deal of practice.

I walked back to the car like John Wayne swaggering off into the sunset, heaved my aching body into the seat, and almost cried at the thought of a hot bath and a good drink. Pretty soon I found out I could start the car but couldn't change from first to second gear or from third to fourth – my arms just didn't want to do any more work. I spent most of the journey avoiding gear changes as much as possible, chugging and spluttering along just like when my Dad taught me to drive. And I was hairy, greasy, and I smelled – worse than I've ever smelled. It was so bad, I drove back with the windows open and the heater on. The following year I got a man in to do the job much quicker and much better than I could ever have managed.

Feeding

Sheep, like goats and cattle, are ruminants – cud-chewing animals. This means they can process foods which other animals cannot – stuff like tough plant material such as grasses and tree branches. Huge quantities can be swallowed with a minimum of chewing; then later, when the animal is resting, it is all regurgitated, rechewed, and broken up into smaller pieces for digestion. All ruminants have four-chambered stomachs; the rumen (hence the name 'ruminant') is the largest, and contains the micro-organisms which secrete enzymes to break down the cellulose in the plant cell walls so that nutrients can be absorbed.

Most of the time, sheep can get all the nutrition they need from the pasture, but during the winter when grazing is poor, hay, silage, root crops or other bagged foods may need to be given as a supplement. At certain times of the year, for example, coming up to tupping (mating), during pregnancy and when ewes are lactating,

If you have a small flock, it makes more sense to hire in a ram.

supplementary feed may be needed. Vitamin and mineral licks – often sold in large tubs – are designed to combat any nutritional deficiencies and can be left out in the fields for sheep to use as needed. A general-purpose high-energy lick is always worth having as a precaution, but others are available for specific purposes. Seek out some of my recommended books below for detailed information on sheep nutritional requirements.

Common health problems
Feet
Probably the biggest problem sheep farmers have is lameness in the flock. If ever God messed up in creating animals, it was with sheep (and goats, for that matter), because their feet have a real design fault. The feet are split into two pads or cleats, and the gap in between them is a lovely warm place where bacteria can lurk and cause foot rot – a painful ailment which is often only spotted when a sheep is seen limping. Although curable, it is better not to have to treat it in the first place, of course. Scald is another uncomfortable condition, caused by long grass irritating the skin between the cleats.

You can't be lazy with footcare. Feet have to be inspected at regular intervals and trimmed as level as possible, otherwise the sheep can get extremely uncomfortable, and this will eventually affect her overall condition. The hooves grow at different rates according to conditions and are affected by weather, terrain, and nutrition. With a small flock, it should be possible to inspect the feet every month or so to keep a check on growth. Once a hoof has started to grow into an awkward shape, it can be difficult or sometimes impossible to correct.

Teeth
Lambs have a full set of 'baby' teeth, and the adult teeth begin to come through around the twelve-month mark, with two erupting in the centre of the bottom jaw. By year two, there will be four prominent teeth, by year three there will be six, and by year four, it will have a complete set of eight fully grown teeth. About two or three years later, the teeth will be showing a great deal of wear and some will have broken or dropped out (hence the expression 'broken-mouthed'. Sheep missing several teeth will not graze well and they soon lose condition. In commercial flocks, ewes are often culled when they get beyond the age of six, or when their teeth indicate they might have difficulty feeding; sheep which can't graze well won't obtain the nutrition to sustain a healthy pregnancy, so aren't commercially viable.

When you have a small flock, however, it's easy to grow attached to ewes and many smallholders allow their old ladies to live out the rest of their days. As long as they don't have to compete for food with others, they should be able to enjoy a good few years more, even if their lamb-bearing days are over.

Worms and other things
Intestinal worms are a common problem for most sheep farmers. All sheep will carry some *roundworms*; eggs get passed out of the body in the faeces; the larvae hatch and

are eaten by other sheep, and they cause sheep to lose condition. Thin and young ewes may need to be drenched (given an oral dose of a wormer) for worms at tupping time, as a precaution, but ewes are generally drenched after lambing. Grazing ewes on clean pasture is the best way of controlling worms, but not always possible. One way of minimizing the risk of infection is to keep just a few sheep per acre. Two to three is generally recommended, but this will vary depending on the type of land and the time of year. Another good practice is to allow grazing on fields in alternate years. A mixed grazing regime – using cattle as well as sheep – can also help reduce the number of larvae which get back into the sheep's body when grazing. The modern approach to worming is only to do so when necessary, as sheep can build up a resistance to drugs used too regularly. However, most farmers will worm as a matter of course when bringing in new sheep, just in case.

Tapeworms live in the small intestine of the sheep and, although they look horrible when excreted, they normally cause little harm to the animal. *Liver fluke* may be a problem in wet and boggy areas. The fluke is a parasite which uses a mud snail as a host to help it reproduce. The immature fluke is found on grass and, when eaten by the sheep, makes its way to the liver, causing severe anaemia, loss of condition and death. *Fly-strike*, as I touched on earlier, is a horrible thing to witness (*see also* Chapter 12). The green or blue blowflies are most active in mild weather, searching for places to lay their eggs. Unsheared sheep are the prime targets, but I've had friends with lambs of just a few weeks old affected. Pour-on insecticides like Vetrazin, Clik or Crovect should be applied as soon as the mild weather begins and the animals should be sheared as soon as is practical to do so. Any open wounds, signs of foot rot or dirty fleeces should be taken care of to prevent the flies being attracted by the smell. Newly hatched maggots waste no time in nibbling their way at the sheep's flesh; the tell-tale signs to watch for include the sheep twisting its head round to try and reach the irritated area; stamping of the hind feet; and the tail wagging frantically. The affected sheep has to be caught, clipped, maggots removed, and the area cleaned and treated. A pour-on product should be applied to deter a secondary strike. Crovect has the advantage that it also kills the maggots when applied to the fly-struck area. Various other preparations are also available which will kill the maggots as well as helping to heal the wound. Maggot oil is a particularly soothing preparation which seems to make affected sheep feel a lot more comfortable.

Scrapie is a fatal viral disease which attacks the brain and the spinal cord and produces a nervous condition. Sheep lose condition along with their fleeces. There is no cure. Official scrapie-monitoring schemes are helping to reduce the spread of the problem, and selective breeding programmes hope eventually to produce stock which are resistant to the virus.

Sheep scab is a highly contagious disease of sheep caused by a mite. Problems are more likely to occur in the winter. Effects include intense irritation, loss of wool, and scabs, and it can lead to death if untreated. It is no longer compulsory to dip sheep in an insecticide as a preventative measure, and instances of the disease are on the

Learning the Lingo: Sheep Jargon

Getting into sheep farming means learning a whole new vocabulary. Here are some of the words and phrases you are most likely to hear.

Broker or broken-mouthed ewe: an ageing sheep with worn or missing teeth

Condition-scoring: examining a sheep to check its growth and suitability for breeding or slaughter

Crutching or dagging: removing soiled wool from a sheep's rear end

Cull ewe: finished ewes sent for slaughter

Draft ewe: usually used to describe ewes which are too old for the rough conditions of hill grazing, but can still be bred from on lower lying land

Drenching: giving oral medicine (e.g. wormer)

Ewe: a mature female

Fat lambs: finished ready for slaughter from three months old onwards

Flushing: increasing the amount of nutrition given prior to mating to improve fertility

Fly-strike: condition caused by maggots eating into the flesh of the sheep after hatching from fly eggs laid in the fleece

Gimmer: used in some areas to describe a young ewe that has not yet had a lamb. 'Chilver' is another expression used

Hogget: a castrated male sheep usually 10 to 14 months old; some use the terms 'hogg' or 'tegg'

Lamb: a young sheep, up to year old; male = ram lamb, female = ewe lamb

Mis-mothering: when a pregnant ewe takes another ewe's lamb

Mutton: the meat of older sheep, generally over 2 years old

Polled: a breed in which horns will not develop

Prolific: used to describe a productive ewe which often produces twins or triplets

Raddle: a harness fitted to a ram before mating which has a pad of coloured dye
The dye rubs off on the ewe's back, so the farmer can tell which ones have been served

Ram: a mature, 'entire' male, i.e. complete with all his important bits and pieces

Shearling or yearling: a sheep which has been sheared once

Store lambs: lambs being fattened for slaughter

Teaser: a vasectomized male (or wether) put into a field with ewes to bring them into season before the fertile ram is brought in

Terminal sire: ram of a breed specially raised for meat, brought in to produce good meat lambs

Tup: a ram kept for breeding

Tupping: mating

Wether: a castrated male

increase. Recent years has seen a move away from dipping and towards more specific injectable treatments.

Vaccination
Many farmers vaccinate sheep annually against a variety of clostridial diseases (infections caused by the clostridia group of bacteria). Others only do so after experiencing a particular problem. Ask your vet for advice on this one.

RECOMMENDED READING
Dave Brown and Sam Meadowcroft, *The Modern Shepherd,* Farming Press, 2002
Mary Castell, *Starting with Sheep,* Broad Leys Publishing, 2003
Eddie Straiton, *Sheep Ailments: Recognition and Treatment,* Crowood Press, 2001
J. Upton and D. Soden, *An Introduction to Keeping Sheep,* Good Life Press, 2007
Agnes Winter, *Lameness in Sheep,* Crowood Press, 2004
—— and Cicely Hill, *A Manual of Lambing Techniques,* Crowood Press, 2003

WEBSITES
www.badgerfacesheep.co.uk Badger Face Sheep Society
www.balwensheepsociety.com Balwen Welsh Mountain Sheep Society
www.beulahsheep.co.uk Beulah Speckled Face Sheep Society
www.blackwelshmountain.org.uk Black Welsh Mountain Sheep Breeders' Association
www.britishwool.org.uk British Wool Marketing Board
www.hillradnor.co.uk Hill Radnor Flock Book Society
www.isds.org.uk International Sheep Dog Society
www.llanwenog-sheep.co.uk Llanwenog Sheep Society
www.lleynsheep.com Lleyn Sheep Society
www.nationalsheep.org.uk National Sheep Association
www.sheepdairying.com British Sheep Dairying Association
www.sheepgame.co.uk Sheep rounding-up game
www.sheepvetsoc.org.uk Sheep Veterinary Society
www.thesheeptrust.org The Sheep Trust

Goats

When I told a friend I was planning to get some goats, he shook his head and said: 'Haven't you heard the old Arab proverb, "Let he who is without problems get a goat"?'

Okay, maybe a tad over the top, but don't underestimate how much work goats demand, nor how stretched your patience will be as a goat keeper trying to stop them wrecking everything in sight. Don't get me wrong – I love goats. Goats are incredibly intelligent, friendly and entertaining. They can be immensely satisfying to keep, and they also have the rather wonderful spin-off benefits of producing milk and meat, and

Goats can be destructive, so protect any precious trees.

fibre for spinning, too. But, rather like a weed is a flower in the wrong place, goats are a nightmare when they are anywhere you don't want them to be. Prepare for total devastation.

Goats were the first four-legged animals to arrive on our smallholding and, in many ways, I felt they marked a turning point in my livestock-keeping; at last, I felt like a 'proper' smallholder. Chickens and other birds are all very well, but having something fairly big, and with a personality to match, can be a real thrill – but also a huge responsibility as well.

As discussed in the previous section about sheep, you'll have to get your holding registered (see Chapter 7), get a flock/herd number – unless you already have one for sheep or cattle – and tag each goat. Movement documents are the same as those for sheep.

Again, you need to ask yourself the question: 'Am I really ready for all this?' Just like sheep, goats need both regular foottrimming and worming, and you'll have to be able to give drugs at some point. You also may have to deliver kids, and learn to milk by hand, so take a good, hard think about this before making an impulse buy.

Your first goats

The more observant of you will notice that I said 'goats' rather than 'goat'. That's because goats are herd animals and therefore need the company of their own kind. Keeping one on its own just isn't fair on the poor animal. Most people start off with two females – a mother and kid, two sisters, or even two which are completely unrelated. As with most animals, there is a definite 'pecking order', and one will inevitably be 'top goat'. You won't be able to change this, so don't try – though you might think about feeding them separately to make sure the bossiest one doesn't eat everything. If you decide later to add another goat or two to the herd, be prepared for some initial problems with bullying, but things will eventually settle down as the new goats find their place in the hierarchy.

My first goats were two female British Alpines – one was about 2 years old and the other a very cute little kid of about 6 months. My intention was to get them both into kid as soon as possible, so that I could start milking them. The plan was to have sufficient milk for the family and, looking to the future, have some to feed to the pigs I would be getting. I also had in mind the idea of mating them with a Boer – a South African goat bred for meat – because I had had a few inquiries about supplying goat meat.

However, like so many great plans, it never happened, and the girls became time-consuming pets – time-consuming because they had to be taken from their shed every morning, led to an area where there was plenty to eat and where they could do no damage, and collected every evening and locked up before dark. They did a fabulous job of clearing the brambles, nettles, and dock, but they took a lot of looking after in return.

I don't believe in tethering animals, so I used battery-operated electric fencing to enclose them during the day. Electric fencing is great when it works, because it allows you to 'strip-graze', moving the animals to a fresh area of ground when they've decimated all vegetation. There are drawbacks with electric fencing, however. Batteries run out unexpectedly and goats are clever enough to work out that when the clicking noise stops there's nothing to fear. I lost count of the number of times the goats wandered up from the bottom fields to the house and wreaked havoc in my flower beds. I was using four parallel strands of electrified tape, threaded through plastic fencing stakes and it took a while to work out how low the bottom strand had to be to stop the goats doing a limbo underneath, and how high the top one had to be to stop them jumping over. Another drawback was that, if the bottom strand was touching wet grass, the fence would short-circuit and be useless.

Goats absolutely hate the rain. A few spots send them scurrying for cover, so when I was strip-grazing, I had to use one of our heavy plastic calf hutches as a makeshift field shelter, moving it to each new location. With hindsight, an easier option might have been using the livestock trailer, which could have been towed. Overnight accommodation also proved a bit of a problem. Goats chew absolutely anything, so my first idea of putting them in a large wooden shed quickly turned out to be a waste of time. They gnawed lumps out of the walls and the door frame and added insult to injury by smashing both windows. For the remainder of their stay, they slept in the livestock trailer, which was at least robust enough to take the pounding they gave it. I eventually came to realize that what we needed was a small concrete stable block surrounded by a courtyard. In the end, I never got round to getting one built – I took the easier option and sold the goats instead.

This young British Alpine goat has a taste for browsing in the garden.

107

Anne Lees, who farms near Caerphilly, recommends British Toggenburgs as reliable milkers.

Secure stock-fencing is vitally important, and you also need to make sure it is high enough to deter your goats from attempting to jump or clamber over. Normal height sheep fencing won't do – they'll be up and over that before you know it – so make it at least 1.2m (4ft) high. Some people suggest putting a strand of barbed wire along the top of normal stock fencing, so the goats are discouraged from resting their feet on the top and working out a plan of escape. Personally, I don't like the idea, because accidents can happen. If a goat is intent on getting out, it may throw caution to the wind, attempt a jump and seriously injure its udder in the process.

Any young or valuable trees you have will need to be protected. My goats nearly wrecked my newly planted orchard when they got in one day. I never forgave them – nor myself for being so negligent. Make a triangular guard around each tree with wooden stakes and strong wire fencing. Also, make sure the guard is high enough to prevent the goats from reaching the lowest branches, because they not only eat them, they also lean on them with their front legs to pull them down to a more convenient position, often snapping whole boughs in the process.

Choosing a breed
If I haven't put you off so far, you're obviously made of sterner stuff than me, so take a look at the different goat breeds, to see which best suits your needs.

Anglo Nubian

Milk from this breed is high in both butterfat and protein, so it is a popular choice with cheese and yoghurt makers. A good dual-purpose (i.e. milk and meat) breed, it has a very distinctive, convex 'Roman' nose and long, droopy ears. The coat is short and silky and comes in a wide range of colours.

Angora

Angoras have long, coarse, curly coats which produce the highly prized mohair. With age, the coat develops 'ringlets' and needs a fair amount of attention to keep in good condition. Angoras are sheared twice a year, so not a breed for the beginner.

Bagot

An ancient British breed with a striking, long black and white coat and an impressive set of large horns. The head and shoulders are black, but everything behind the shoulders is white. A nervous breed, so not recommended for the beginner.

Boer

A specialist meat breed from South Africa, it is white with a reddish-brown head, floppy ears and a strong, muscular body. They produce less milk than other breeds, but are still a good dual-purpose choice. Males can weigh as much as 150kg (330lb).

British Alpine

Good milkers, British Alpines have predominantly black coats, with white face, legs, and tail markings. It has what is described as a 'rangy' build, quite angular in appearance and very impressive when the coat is in good, glossy condition.

British Saanen

Probably the most popular milking breed because of yield and length of lactation. These white goats have an easy-going nature, so a good choice for beginners. Saanens are often used as foundation stock in commercial farms and cross-bred with other breeds.

British Toggenburg

The Toggenburg looks like a British Alpine in colour! The Alpine white markings are the same, but the Toggenburg is predominantly brown. One of the most popular breeds, and a favourite with cheese makers.

Golden Guernsey

Beautiful golden-coated breed, with some variations in shade, and coats of varying lengths. Good, quiet temperament, and one of the smaller dairy breeds, so easier to handle. There is also a British Guernsey, which looks the same, but is larger. *(continued)*

Pygmy goats

Just like bantams in chicken breeds, these are miniature versions which are very popular pets. Much easier to handle, they are a good choice for children or if you have a limited amount of space and accommodation available. The Pygmy Goat Club stipulates that a male pygmy should be no more than 56cm at the withers; females are smaller still.

Incidentally, if you're heard people talk of 'cashmere goats' and are wondering why these aren't included in the list, it is because there is no cashmere breed. Cashmere is the soft, downy layer of insulating hair which grows underneath the main outer coat. Normally, this is just moulted in spring, but many people harvest it by combing and use it for spinning.

Finding your goats

Agricultural shows are excellent places for getting to know about goats and meeting breeders face-to-face. Goat breeders are always happy to chat about their animals and to give advice to newcomers, so don't be afraid to ask. Once you've decided the kind of goats would you like to own, talking to owners or getting in touch with the breed society will help you find a breeder near you. You may also find a local goat club in the area. The British Goat Society (see details at the end of this section) has contact details for all the breed societies.

Ideal for a beginner, pygmy goats like these at the Machen Show are easy to handle.

When you come to viewing potential purchases, perform the same general health checks you would for any animal, as outlined earlier in this chapter. Of course, if you've done as I suggested and have tracked down a reputable breeder, you should be in safe hands, as a good breeder won't risk reputation by selling poor stock. Before you take your goats away, ask the breeder to run through basic husbandry tasks, like foot-trimming, giving wormer and milking. Another thing you should definitely do is have your goats' accommodation and feeding equipment ready before they arrive. Goats are impatient beasts at the best of times, so don't keep them waiting!

Feeding

A balanced diet and constant supply of fresh water are the essentials when it comes to keeping goats – and all other animals, for that matter. Just like sheep and cattle, goats are ruminants, so they take in lots of tough old stuff very quickly and deal with it later (refer back to the sheep section).

As we've already discussed, goats are browsers by nature, and love nothing more than foraging for their own food. The way they have evolved over the years means they need a huge amount of bulky feed, and at least half of their daily diet should be made up of forage alone. If they can't be left to fend for themselves and hunt down their own tree branches and vegetation, to satisfy their mineral and roughage requirements, they will need good hay and silage (preferably maize silage), supplemented with a good goat mix containing ingredients like maize, oats, barley, wheat, beans, peas, etc. I always preferred coarse mixes over pelleted ones, but the drawback is that some goats are a bit fussy, and pick out only the bits they like, and so may miss out on certain nutrients. Pellets are a 'one-stop shop'.

My goats had the luxury of being able to wander around and feed themselves, but they always had about a cupful of commercial goat food each day, sometimes more if I thought grazing was poor. Had I got them into kid, I would have increased the amount of supplementary food accordingly during late pregnancy and throughout the time they were producing milk. There are some excellent books on the market which will give you detailed instructions on what and how much to feed at various times of a goat's life, so see the recommended titles at the end of this section.

If you are letting your goats browse naturally, be aware that some plants and trees can be poisonous – the best-known include rhododendron, yew, laurel and bracken. Most of the time, goats seem to instinctively know what to eat and what to avoid – more so than other livestock – but it pays to be wary on their behalf. Many experienced goat keepers say it is best to regard all cultivated (i.e. non-native) garden plants as potential-ly toxic – so keep your goats out of your flower beds.

Accommodation

The first golden rule is to find a place which is dry and free from draughts; goats cope well in cold weather, but they hate being wet or in draughty conditions. Ideally, the housing should lead out onto a yard or a field so that the goats can be easily let out for exercise – otherwise you'll have to do as I did and attach dog leads to their collars and lead them to and from their foraging area twice a day. Be warned that goats are extremely clever, and they quickly learn how to open latches and even bolts. I've seen them do this, and it's quite remarkable, so make sure your doors are securely locked on the outside.

Safety has to come first, so the shed or building you intend using must be free from sharp edges, and the same goes for fittings. Similarly, take care when positioning hay to avoid injury, particularly to the eyes. Hay nets shouldn't be used for goats with horns or for young kids, as they could get tangled. Check that the interior of the building is not covered with lead paint, or any other paint or wood preservative which could be toxic to your goats.

The space devoted to food and water also needs careful consideration. Goats should have sufficient space to feed without having to push one another out of the way (although this will probably happen when the lead goat finishes her food). Water troughs or buckets should be positioned so that they can't be contaminated by drop-pings. One of the best ideas I've seen is a simple bucket-holder (available by mail order from smallholding suppliers like Ascott, *www.ascott.biz* or tel. 0845 130 6285) which can be fixed onto a wall or door safely out of the line of fire.

Dry bedding – such as straw or bark chippings – is essential and must be changed regularly; solid floors should be well-drained, because goats – even if only housed overnight – can wee to championship standard. Damp floors can harbour bacteria which can cause foot rot, which can lead to lameness. If you're planning to milk your goats, you will also need a separate area for milking, which must be well-ventilated and easy to clean. Food safety laws are strict, and if you intend selling your milk – even on a small scale – your premises will have to be inspected and registered before you can begin trading.

Do I need a billy goat?
The sensible answer is a loud, resounding 'No!' Refer back to the section on hens and cockerels, and the same things apply. Unless you get seriously into the breeding side of things, don't bother. If you need one for mating, find an experienced local breeder and take your goats to be served. Entire (uncastrated) male goats are more trouble than they are worth; they can be difficult to handle and aggressive and they stink, too, particularly in the mating season. From late summer to about March, protective clothes need to be worn because the smell clings incredibly well to skin and clothing alike. Lovely.

Potential problems and things to remember
Goats share a wide variety of health problems with sheep. They need regular worming, their feet need regular trimming to prevent lameness, they can pick up parasites like ticks, fleas and lice, and they can suffer from mastitis – a bacterial infection that causes lumps in the udder which must be treated with antibiotics. See the section on sheep in this chapter for more information.

Feeding must be carried out with care. Make sure that you don't overfeed certain foods, for example, concentrates, which can lead to digestive problems like bloating, acidosis and laminitis. Overfeeding can, of course, cause obesity. As well as being very bad for the general health of the animal, this can also cause problems when trying to get a female into kid.

Disbudding should be carried out within the first ten days of birth – ideally within the first two to three days. It should not be attempted by an amateur, so ask for veterinary advice.

If you don't want to breed from your male kids – or if you're rearing them for meat – they need to be castrated. This can be done, as with lambs, using a specially designed rubber ring and applicator, but it must be done by an experienced person, and within the first few weeks of life. Kids over 2 months old should only be castrated under anaesthetic and by a veterinary surgeon.

FURTHER INFORMATION
British Goat Society, tel. 01626 833168 (*www.allgoats.com*)

RECOMMENDED READING
David Harwood, *Goat Health and Welfare*, Crowood Press, 2006
Ulrich Jaudas, *The New Goat Handbook*, Barrons, 1989
David Mackenzie, *Goat Husbandry*, Faber & Faber, 1993
Alan Mowlem, *Practical Goatkeeping*, Crowood Press, 2001
Katie Thear, *Starting with Goats*, Broad Leys Publishing, 2006

BREED SOCIETIES
www.anglo-nubian.org.uk Anglo Nubian Breed Society
www.bagot-goat.freeserve.co.uk Bagot Goat Breed Society
www.britishalpines.co.uk British Alpine Breed Society
www.britishangoragoats.org.uk British Angora Goat Society
www.britishboergoatsociety.co.uk British Boer Goat Society
www.britishtoggenburgs.co.uk British Toggenburg Society
www.goldenguernseygoat.org.uk Golden Guernsey Goat Society
www.npga-pygmy.com National Pygmy Goat Association
www.pygmygoatclub.org Pygmy Goat Club

Pigs

I've been fascinated by pigs ever since I was a child growing up in Merthyr Tydfil and I saw an enormous runaway sow which had escaped from a farm wandering around the terraced streets of Dowlais. Seeing a pig outdoors – let alone in the high street – in those days was as rare as seeing a zebra in the corner shop. At that time (in the 1960s)

Tiny piglets can be extremely endearing, but they soon grow – so make sure you have got the space to accommodate them and the strength needed for handling.

most pork was reared intensively indoors, and no one ever used the expression 'free-range'. Happily, more and more people are coming round to the idea that the best way to rear pigs is the natural way, though it will be a long while before the sight of fields and woodlands full of pigs becomes a familiar one.

Gerry will tell you I started going at him about getting pigs soon after we got our smallholding. I bought all the books and I joined the Wales and Border Counties Pig Breeders' Association two years before getting my first pigs. I got to know lots of breeders, tried different types of pork, and swotted up on everything I needed to know. By the time the land was properly stock-fenced, water piped to each field and ready to accept pigs, I felt fairly knowledgeable.

Pigs must be the most rewarding of livestock to keep. First, they are highly intelligent. Winston Churchill famously acknowledged this when he said: 'Cats look down on you; dogs look up to you; but pigs look you in the eye as equals.' Similarly, G. K. Chesterton enthused: 'Pigs are very beautiful animals. Those who think otherwise are those who do not look at anything with their own eyes, but only with other people's eyeglasses.' And Harry S. Truman said: 'No man should be allowed to be president who does not understand pigs, or hasn't been around a manure pile.'

The fact that pigs are so bright, entertaining and much easier to bond with than any other animals can pose a bit of a problem, as some people find they get far too attached and can't bear to part with them when they reach slaughter weight. Consequently, there are a lot of smallholders around with expensive, ageing pet pigs. Pig-keeping has definitely undergone something of a renaissance. It has never been so popular or so fashionable – largely due to TV chefs like Gordon Ramsay and Hugh Fearnley-Whittingstall convincing the viewing public that there is nothing better than home-reared pork.

Starting off

So how easy is it to keep pigs? Well, if you take the simple route – as I've been advising all along in this introduction to keeping livestock – and buy in a couple of weaners to fatten, it can be fairly straightforward. You will, of course, have to have your holding number and herd number sorted out in advance and order some ear tags (see Chapter 7 for details). You will obviously need to do your research, find out as much as you can from breeders and get your accommodation in order before you start. One thing you should consider is whether you are ready to take on pigs.

Any animal reared from weaning age – the age of separation from the mother, which is normally about 8 to 10 weeks – which has daily contact with you is likely to grow into a friendly and sociable creature which should be easy to handle. However, cute little weaners quickly grow into big, strong pigs and, as they are so incredibly food-driven, they can quite happily knock you flying in order to get to the bag of food you're carrying. You will have to satisfy yourself that you – or a companion – are strong enough to handle pigs. Even if you are just fattening for the abattoir, you will still have to put metal tags in their ears before they go off, and that means holding still what might be a 70kg animal while you do the business.

Pigs also have teeth and big, strong jaws. They won't necessarily mean to nip you, but they do have a tendency to sniff and nibble at anything to check if it's edible. The heels of my wellies are testament to that. For this reason, visitors, children and dogs should never be allowed in with them unsupervised.

Buying in weaners like these to fatten is a good way to start with pigs.

Help from the experts

A really good investment of a few pounds a year is membership of the Wales and Border Counties Pig Breeders' Association. Don't be put off by the title, because it's not just for breeders; many of the members simply buy in pigs for fattening, while others don't have any pigs, but have an interest in them and enjoy the social side of the association. At the heart of the organization are the best breeders in the country, and their advice and guidance is second to none.

For your annual membership fee, you get a directory which lists breeders, abattoirs, butchers, smokeries, suppliers of agricultural feed and equipment, details of farmers' markets and an invaluable gestation table, which (should you progress to breeding) allows you to calculate when your girls will farrow. There is also a quarterly newsletter which contains, among other things, classified ads for stock, services, feed and equipment.

The association always has a stand at the Royal Welsh Smallholder and Garden Festival (May), the Royal Welsh Agricultural Show (July) and the Royal Welsh Winter Fair (December). The members work really hard at both events to organize competitions and displays of handling – including the hilarious 'pig agility' challenge, where owners attempt to shepherd their pigs around an assault course. For details of how to join ring chairman Keith Brown on 01982 552100 or visit *www.pigsonline.org.uk*.

Beauty is in the eye of the beholder: two of the Tamworths of top breeder Barbara Warren.

Your first weaners

Most breeders will encourage you to buy your weaners in spring. Not only is it much nicer looking after your pigs in good weather, it also makes good economic sense, because in winter, some of the food you give them will be utilized to keep them warm. Saying that, I got my first pigs in November, but they still did really well – and it was an incredible bonus seeing ginger Tamworths running around in the snow!

Different people rear their pigs in different ways. Naturally, the old traditional breeds are slower growing than the commercial types which have been selectively bred to mature quickly and therefore keep rearing costs down. It's up to you. Do you want cheap, ultra-lean pork, or do you want pork which takes longer to produce and costs a bit more, but has a good layer of fat, and an excellent flavour?

There is also the aesthetic aspect to consider. It may sound weird, but I get a kick out of seeing nice pigs. Golden pigs glistening in the sun against a lush green backdrop is a scene which is difficult to improve. Barbara Warren, the woman who has probably taught me more about pigs than I could ever have learned from books, calls it the 'tingle factor'. She reckons that, when choosing a breed, you should go for the ones that give you that special feeling inside when you look at them. Some people favour lop-eared pigs over prick-eared ones because a pig whose sight is partly obscured by floppy ears is regarded as more docile, whereas the other lot, which have ears standing up to attention, can see where they're going and waste no time in going there.

As with the previous livestock discussed, I'm assuming you're going to rear your pigs outdoors. I make no apology for this. I think it's a basic right of livestock to live in as natural surroundings as possible; while my pigs are with me, they have a wonderful life and they deserve it. With this in mind, you should be looking for a breed which is well-suited to the free-range lifestyle, and you need look no further than the traditional breeds.

Accommodation

In my grandmother's day, a pig in the back garden was a common sight. One of the great things for the smallholder is that pigs don't need a huge amount of space compared with, for instance, sheep or cattle. Saying that, however, I like mine to have plenty of space to run about, so I keep them in paddocks of about half an acre to an acre in size, moving them on when they root up the ground to such an extent that it looks like the Somme. In some ways, giving them lots of room to run around is as much for my benefit as it is for theirs; watching your pigs racing about or wallowing contentedly in mud is a wonderful thing.

Shelter from the sun as well as the wind and rain is vitally important. One of the big dangers with pigs is overheating, so you should aim to provide shading and a mud wallow in the paddock. Pigs can suffer from heat stress, sunburn and sunstroke, so be warned. My pigs live all year round in purpose-built arks which have timber floors and corrugated metal roofs, but I've seen home-made alternatives made of wooden pallets, straw bales or old shed doors. Other people use plastic calf hutches and even dog

The Breeds

Berkshire
Don't be put off by the black coat of the Berkshire – the meat and the rind is white. The black colour gene is recessive, so Berkshires cross-bred with white pigs will produce white piglets. The breed is quick to reach slaughter weight, so economical to rear. They do well outdoors, withstanding extremes of temperature all year round. Classed as 'vulnerable' by the Rare Breeds Survival Trust (RBST).

British landrace
One of the UK's most popular commercial breeds in the UK, renowned for its lean carcase. Originally imported from Sweden, this white pig is the most frequently used by commercial producers for crossing with other breeds.

British lop
Closely related to the Welsh and the landrace, this is a white pig with long, lean sides. The big lop ears make it docile and easy to handle, and it is a good choice for outdoor rearing. Classed as 'endangered' by the RBST.

British saddleback
This breed is the result of crossing the Essex (brought to the public's attention by the BBC TV series *Jimmy's Farm*) and the Wessex saddleback. The markings are black with a wide band or saddle of white over the shoulders and the forelegs. Hardy and good at foraging. Classed as 'at risk' by the RBST.

Duroc
A deep red pig, originally from the USA. Quick to mature, it has a deep, muscular body and broad hams and shoulders. Popular for crossing with other breeds.

Gloucestershire old spots
This is the original 'orchard pig', traditionally reared on windfall apples and whey. A white pig with black spots, folklore says that the spots were caused by falling apples! Hardy and very popular with smallholders, it is still a 'minority' breed, in relatively low numbers.

Hampshire
At first glance, similar in appearance to the British saddleback, this breed is black with a white saddle around the shoulders and forelegs. Unlike the saddleback, it has pricked ears. Originally from Wessex, the Hampshire was developed in the USA and is considered by many to be the best terminal sire breed – i.e. the best boar for crossing with other breeds.

Large black
A large but docile lop-eared breed, this is the only all-black pig native to the UK. Its colouring helps it resist sunburn, so it does well outdoors in summer. These pigs are long with deep sides and are classed as 'vulnerable' by the RBST.

Middle white
Beauty is in the eye of the beholder, and I'm afraid I think this is the ugliest breed of pig. It has a squashed or 'dished' face – a legacy from cross-breeding with Asian pigs – which makes it unmistakable from any other breed. The patron of the Middle White Pig Breeders' Club is celebrity chef Antony Worrall Thompson, who bears a striking resemblance to his favourite breed. An early maturing breed which is classed as 'endangered' by the RBST.

Oxford sandy and black
One of the oldest British pig breeds, having been around for up to 300 years, this is often described as the traditional farmers' and cottagers' pig. It bears some resemblance to the Berkshire and Tamworth; the head and ears are similar to the Berkshire, while the coat is Tamworth ginger with black spots. The breed is docile, hardy, and loves foraging.

Pietrain
This breed takes its name from the village of Pietrain in Belgium, where it developed. White with black spots, it produces very lean meat. Extremely popular for crossing with other breeds to improve the carcase.

Tamworth
The most primitive-looking of the UK breeds, the Tamworth has a distinctive ginger coat, long snout, and prick ears. The Tamworth was considered a poor choice for cross-breeding when Asian pigs started to be introduced into many pigs' bloodlines. It is therefore the purest of the British breeds and the closest living relative of the original forest pig. Classed as 'vulnerable' by the RBST.

Welsh
The only indigenous Welsh breed, this is a white pig with lop ears which almost meet at the nose. It has a long, level body and deep, strong hams. Around fifty years ago, the Welsh was one of the most popular breeds in the UK, widely used in commercial herds and cross-breeding. Beginning to enjoy something of a resurgence, thanks to a small number of dedicated breeders. Classed as 'vulnerable' by the RBST.

A Berkshire pig takes to the ring at the Royal Welsh Agricultural Show with handler Chris Impey.

kennels. Of course, if you have stables or other outbuildings, these can be adapted, too. As long the accommodation you choose is dry, draught-free and filled with plenty of straw, your pigs should be snug and warm. If you want to buy an off-the-peg ark, there are always plenty of advertisements in magazines like *Country Smallholding and Smallholder*, and most good agricultural shows attract at least one or two suppliers.

The way you site your ark is important. Make sure the entrance faces away from the prevailing wind, and suspend strips of heavy, see-through plastic from above the entrance to create a curtain effect which will help cut down draughts. Pigs are really clean animals, and tend not to use their sleeping quarters as a toilet, so clearing out your ark shouldn't be too unpleasant. The one thing you can't teach them, however, is to wipe their feet, so in wet, muddy conditions you'll find the bedding needs renewing frequently.

Feeding

Pigs seem to live just to eat, and you can be sure that if you overdo planting up the veg patch nothing will go to waste. Years ago, pigs used to double up as waste disposal units, being fed anything and everything that was left over at mealtimes. it was customary to keep a 'swill bucket' in the kitchen to collect any scraps rinsed off plates. This is no longer possible. Since 2001 – during the foot-and-mouth epidemic – it has been illegal to give pigs waste food. A national ban on giving food containing meat was introduced as an emergency measure during the outbreak because it was feared the virus could be in circulation in meat. Later, the ruling was reinforced by the Animal By-Products Regulations 2005, which define catering waste as '*all* waste food, including used cooking oil originating in restaurants, catering facilities and kitchens, including central kitchens and household kitchens'. In short, nothing from your kitchen – or anyone else's – can be fed to pigs. Anyone in breach could face either a fine or even imprisonment.

By far the easiest way to feed your pigs is to give them a commercial ration which has been carefully blended to contain all the nutrients they need to grow well. Pelleted food, called pig 'nuts' or 'rolls', normally contain a variety of cereal crops and are made with specific stages of the growing phase in mind – from weaner age to 'finishing' age. As with most animals, weaners require a higher level of protein in their food, and the level should be decreased as they get older. Everyone has their own way of feeding, but the table shows what I give mine, along with any spare fruit and veg.

Table II. Rearing for pork

Approximate age in weeks	Food per day*
8	1.5lb / 0.7kg
12	2.5lb/ 1.1kg
16	3.5lb/ 1.6kg
18	3lb /1.4kg
20	3lb /1.4kg
24	3lb /1.4kg

This is split into two feeds

Pigs reared for meat have their feed reduced to 3lb (1.4kg) at 18 weeks (when they start to lay down fat) and are kept on this maintenance diet until slaughter at about 24 weeks, to prevent them putting on too much weight. If I was rearing for bacon, I would keep them on the same ration until they were about 36 weeks.

I split the daily feed ration into two portions, to avoid bloating and scouring (diarrhoea). It also gives the pigs something to look forward to twice a day, and means that I have more chance of spotting changes in behaviour and potential problems. Personally, I prefer to feed by scattering the food evenly across the ground, so that all the pigs have a good chance of getting all they need to eat. This is fine as long as the ground is dry; I do tend to use a trough if the ground gets really muddy. The thing to bear in mind about trough-feeding is that, as well as keeping the trough clean, you should ensure it is big enough to allow all your animals to feed at the same time. If not, fights will break out, the trough will more than likely be overturned, and the less forceful pigs will be pushed out of the way.

Water

The importance of water should not be forgotten. You'll be surprised how much a pig can drink during a day – often as much as 10 litres for an adult. The best thing Gerry and I ever did for our livestock was to invest in plastic trough drinkers which refill themselves. They're fairly cheap to buy and, once they're connected to the water supply, your worries about pigs going thirsty are over – unless, of course, they manage to disconnect the pipe, knock over the drinking bath, or wreck it completely by trying to climb inside! With weaners, make sure that whatever you use as a water container isn't so deep that they can fall inside and drown. We use shallow containers until the weaners are big and strong enough to be given access to the automatic drinkers.

Time to go: deciding when to book the abattoir

No one wants to think about this bit when just starting off with a cute pair of weaners, but you have to plan ahead. Rare breed pigs like my Tamworths are slower growing than commercial breeds, and don't normally reach the weight at which they will be slaughtered for pork until about 24 weeks. Some people get them up to weight sooner, but I don't like to rush things, and the quality of the pork we have been getting back has been phenomenal.

Commercial breeds and cross-breeds grow much faster and may get to pork weight as early as 14 weeks. One way to judge whether your pigs are ready is to use a special

The Welsh pig was once so rare that it was in danger of dying out, but numbers are starting to recover thanks to dedicated Welsh breeders.

Learning the Lingo: Pig Jargon

Just like sheep farmers, pig-keepers have a vocabulary all of their own. Here are some of the words and phrases you are most likely to hear.

Bacon: cured pigmeat
Baconer: a pig being reared for bacon rather than pork, and which will be slaughtered between 80 and 100kg
Boar: an uncastrated male pig over six months of age
Gestation period: length of pregnancy, which is three months, three weeks, three days
Gilt: a young female pig which has not yet produced a litter
Hog: castrated male pig
Piglet: young pig
Pork: fresh, uncured pigmeat
Porker: a pig reared to pork weight (normally around 60kg), rather than bacon weight
Stores: pigs which are being fattened for meat
Sow: a female pig after she has had her first litter
Weaner: a piglet separated from its mother and eating solid food. Weaning normally takes place between five and ten weeks

kind of tape measure called a weigh band or weight band, which measures the size in pounds and kilos instead of inches and centimetres. As a general rule, pigs intended for pork are considered ready between about 50kg and 65kg (110lb to 147lb). Note that this refers to the live weight – you'll obviously get less back from the butcher. A slight complication that I found with Tamworths is that, because their shape is different to most pigs, adjustments have to be made when using a weigh band. I was told to measure and then take away 6kg to allow for the difference.

Bringing home the bacon
Rearing pigs for bacon is a bit more complex. First of all, traditional pigs will be about nine months old when they are ready. Now, bearing in mind that boars reaching maturity can tend to be a bit frisky and sometimes a bit boisterous around this age, is it any surprise that most people who rear for bacon choose gilts? There's no hard and fast rule, but there is a considerable debate about the effect that the male hormones can have on the flavour of the meat. Some people say that there can be a definite 'boar taint' to older meat, while others say it's all in the imagination. I spoke to two pig breeders who sent off uncastrated (or 'entire') boars aged just over 12 months and 2 years old respectively for slaughter, and both said the meat was excellent, with no hint of a taint.

That said, however, why put yourself through the hassle of keeping hold of an unruly boar for longer than you have to? Probably best to go for the easier option and choose some gilts if you have bacon in mind. Make sure, however, that you have a butcher who can cure the meat for you. Sadly, just as so many village butchers are disappearing, so are those with the skills to produce their own bacon, so find someone before you commit yourself – or get on a course and learn how to make your own!

Potential problems and common ailments

As with most animals, there are some really scary-sounding diseases and ailments described in the pig-keeping textbooks. However, if you are buying in weaners to fatten and apply good husbandry, you shouldn't have to worry too much. It pays, of course, to be aware of what's out there, so get yourself some of the books mentioned in the list below which go into much more detail.

I mentioned earlier that heat-related health problems (e.g. heat stress, sunburn and sunstroke) can occur in the summer months. Prevention is the best course of action, so make sure your pigs are well-sheltered, well-watered and, if possible, have a good mud wallow available. Mange and lice can be found on even the healthiest pigs. Mange is caused by a burrowing mite which works its way under the skin. The skin gets red and starts to wrinkle, eventually developing crusts. This result is severe irritation, and growth rates can be affected. Lice are fairly big and can be seen crawling on the skin. They suck blood and can cause anaemia and transmit infections. Large-scale producers will vaccinate as a precaution, but I've never done so as a preventative measure because I haven't so far had any problems. Intestinal worms can slow down growth rates. Regular worming and good hygiene – including moving pigs to new pasture and allowing ground to rest – helps keep problems to a minimum.

Pigs will have a go at eating practically anything, so it makes sense to keep anything inedible – such as discarded rubbish – or anything believed to be poisonous well out of their reach. Plants like foxgloves, hemlock, laburnum and yew are well known as dangerous to livestock, so check the paddock regularly. Watch out for greedy pigs overdoing it on fallen acorns, which can cause stomach problems, and even make sows abort. Another thing to be wary of is allowing your pigs to forage unchecked in an orchard. Windfalls eaten by pigs can start fermenting and cause drunkenness (honestly!) and stomach problems.

FURTHER INFORMATION

Wales and Border Counties Pig Breeders' Association, tel. 01982 552100
    (*www.pigsonline.org.uk*)
British Pig Association, tel. 0870 4443906 (*www.britishpigs.org*)

RECOMMENDED READING

Andy Case, *Starting with Pigs,* Broad Leys Publishing, 2001
Maynard Davies, *Maynard, Adventures of a Bacon Curer,* Merlin Unwin Books, 2003
— *Maynard, Secrets of a Bacon Curer,* Merlin Unwin Books, 2007

Elisabeth Downing, *Keeping Pigs,* Pelham Books, 1989
Lyall Watson, *The Whole Hog: Exploring the Extraordinary Potential of Pigs,* Profile Books, 2005
Mark White, *Pig Ailments: Recognition and Treatment,* Crowood Press, 2005

BREED SOCIETIES

www.berkshirepigs.org.uk Berkshire Pig Breeders' Club
www.britishkunekunepigsociety.co.uk British Kune Kune Pig Society
www.britishloppig.org.uk British Lop Pig Society
www.britishpigs.org.uk British Pig Association
largeblackpig.com Large Black Pig Breeders' Club
www.middle-white-pigs.co.uk Middle White Pigs
www.npa-uk.net National Pig Association
www.oldspots.org.uk Gloucestershire Old Spot Breeders Club
www.oxfordsandypigs.co.uk Oxford Sandy and Black Pig Society
www.pigsinwoodlands.co.uk Pigs in Woodlands Association
www.saddlebacks.org.uk British Saddleback Breeders' Club
www.tamworthbreedersclub.co.uk Tamworth Breeders' Club
www.thepigsite.com The Pig Site

Cattle

So goats don't appeal to you? Or is it that you fancy getting into butter, cheese, yoghurt, or beef production? I must admit, I do like cows, and I'm often taken aback at the beauty of Highland cattle at the agricultural shows, but I can't see me taking the plunge and keeping them myself in the foreseeable future. Quite simply, I haven't got the ground to spare, nor the time for hand-milking twice a day. Also, as I already buy excellent beef from our neighbour, there's little point in going to all the trouble of rearing my own for meat.

Cows, in my opinion, are immensely high-maintenance – in financial, physical, and emotional terms. I know many smallholders who already keep them may disagree with me, but I feel they are way beyond the capabilities of the average newcomer to livestock-keeping. Feel free to prove me wrong if you wish, but don't say I didn't warn you! Another downside to keeping cattle is that there are far more health and movement regulations to obey, and mountains more paperwork and inspections involved. Keeping cattle is an increasingly complex business, and I take my hat off to those who do it.

For these reasons, I'm not going to dwell too much on them in this book. If you want to do further research, I've listed what I believe are some of the best books around. Many of my friends have cattle and say there's nothing more rewarding. Personally, I'd recommend that if you need cattle to graze your land, or you merely like the idea of seeing cows through the window, put the word around and see how many farmers come running when they know there is spare grazing available.

Highland cattle are real head-turners, but they may be too ambitious for beginners.

Dexters: a breed for the smallholder

People choose to keep cattle for milk and for beef. Some breeds have been developed particularly for dairy production (for example, Friesian, Holstein, Ayrshire, Guernsey, Jersey), and there are those which are favoured for beef (for example, Welsh black, Hereford, Aberdeen Angus). Saying that, however, around three-quarters of beef produced in the UK comes from dairy cattle.

Smallholders who are hell-bent on keeping a 'house-cow' are often advised to go for dexters. Jerseys are also frequently suggested, because of their docile nature, smaller milk yield and particularly rich milk in comparison to other dairy breeds. The downside of Jerseys is that, because they are dairy cows, any calves they have won't have much meat on them, unless crossed with a suitable bull bred for meat rather than milk.

The dexter is the smallest British breed of cattle – about half the size of a Hereford for example – and stands around a metre high at the shoulder. It is described as a 'dual-purpose' breed – equally capable of providing good milk and good meat – and, because of its size (between 300 and 350kg), considered easier to handle than larger breeds. It comes in three colours (black, red and dun) and there are short-legged and longer legged types.

Dexters are said to be economical to raise. One factor is that the heifers mature young and can be put to the bull at 15–18 months of age. They are noted for their longevity, too, and, according to the Dexter Cattle Society of Great Britain, have been known to breed for fourteen years or more. Average carcase weights range from 145 to 220kg, with a good meat-to-bone ratio. Dexter meat is very popular with people who want small joints, so it sells well at farmers' markets. Originally from south-west Ireland, dexters are hardy and good outdoors all year round. Because they are light-footed, they have proved popular right across the UK for use in conservation grazing schemes where heavier cattle would not be suitable.

Penny Hurt and Chris Bruce have a 15-acre smallholding near Clyro Hill in Radnorshire, mid-Wales, and are dexter devotees. 'We find dexters friendly and inquisitive,' Penny explains. 'They are very amenable to being led by the bucket, but they can be quite frisky, and you need good handling facilities, as with all cattle. Dexters need their feet trimmed every year, so we bought a cattle crush even though we only have a few, and it makes life much easier. You also need good fences – especially at weaning time, as we've found out to our cost!'

Movement regulations

Cattle are slightly more complicated creatures to move than sheep, goats or pigs. You'll be dealing with the British Cattle Movement Society instead of trading standards, and each animal must have an individual passport (see Chapter 7).

Dexters are a popular choice with smallholders but, warns Penny Hurt, they can be frisky.

Accommodation

Dexters are compact little things, and it is generally accepted that you can accommodate two on the amount of land you would normally devote to one standard-size cow. Most of the textbooks will tell you that one standard cow requires an acre (0.4ha) of good grazing land, so you could get two dexters to an acre. This, however, depends on the quality of the land, the weather and other conditions. If your land gets incredibly boggy, for instance, you're going to have far less good-quality grass available.

You will need a good field shelter to protect your animals from the elements, and you're also likely – unless you have spectacularly good stock-fencing – to need electric fencing to keep your cattle from wandering where they shouldn't. Most commercial farmers take their cattle indoors by about October or November and often don't turn them back out to grass until April, or even May in some places. This protects them from the worst of the weather, helps keep milk yields up in dairy cattle and rests the ground when it is at its most vulnerable; seriously poached ground means next year's grass will be disappointing.

A lot of dexter breeders keep their cattle outside all year round. Assess the pros and cons of doing this on your smallholding and ask for advice from experienced breeders if you're unsure what to do. If your cattle will be indoors over winter, make sure you have decent, water-tight, well-ventilated and well-lit outbuildings. If in doubt about their suitability, ask a farming neighbour or your vet for advice. Don't underestimate the work involved in looking after cattle over winter. Remember, their accommodation will need constant mucking out and you're going to be using a huge quantity of straw or other materials for bedding.

Feeding

Grass is the cheapest food but you will only be able to rely on it from spring to autumn. The rest of the time you'll need to feed hay or silage – bought in from others or produced on your holding earlier in the year – or provide purpose-made concentrated food. Don't forget the water! A cow can drink about 30 litres a day – more in hot weather – so it pays to have automatic drinkers set up – or a good family rota for refilling the troughs.

Keeping dexters for milk

Raising cattle for meat is one thing, but if you want milk as well, you're entering a whole new, complicated world. So far, when talking about the various animals you might consider keeping, I've consciously kept away from talking about the ins and outs of breeding. I'm not going to treat this section any differently. What I will say is that, if you want a cow you can milk, you have to get into the breeding side of things.

It's amazing how many people don't realize that, to keep a cow milking, she has to keep calving. Maybe they get confused because goats are often able to go for several years between kids without losing their milk. Human mothers, too, can carry on breast-feeding for as long as five years, sometimes more – though their sanity should be questioned, in my opinion.

Learning the Lingo: Cattle Jargon

Bull: an entire (uncastrated) male of breeding age, usually over a year old
Bullock: a mature castrated male destined for meat production
Calf: a bovine animal less than a year old
Bull calf: entire male young animal up to stage of yearling
Dairy cow: a breed specifically bred for milk production
Cow: a mature female which has had one calf
Cull cow: a cow slaughtered out of the herd
Dry cow: a mature cow which is not lactating
Fat stock/finished stock: beef animals ready for slaughter
Freemartin: a female born with a male twin, usually infertile
Heifer: a young female up to birth of her first calf or in lactation following the first calving
Maiden heifer/bulling heifer: a heifer before going the bull
Steer: a castrated male animal over one year of age
Store cattle: beef cattle reared on more than one farm, and then sold on
Yearling: an animal in its second year of age

It is normal to have one calf a year, so you need to think about where you're going to get your hands on a bull, or an artificial insemination (AI) person. Dexters are said to have trouble-free births, but you will still have to know what to do in an emergency, and how to care for the calf once it's born, so get trained up before you even think about getting your cow into calf.

When the whole, messy business is over, there's also the little matter of weaning the calf and getting to grips with milking by hand. Your cow is going to need to be milked twice a day, and she won't appreciate it if, one day, you fancy an extra hour or two in bed. Make sure you can cope with the technique of milking, have the required facilities, and – just as importantly – have a relief milker or two lined up, just in case you can't do it on occasions.

FURTHER INFORMATION

British Cattle Movement Society, tel. 0845 050 1234, Welsh 0845 050 3456 (*www.bcms.gov.uk*)
Dexter Cattle Society of Great Britain, tel. 02476 692300 (*www.dextercattle.co.uk*)
Dexter Cattle for Sale, tel. 01509 211864 evenings or weekends only
  (*www.dextercattleforsale.co.uk*)

RECOMMENDED READING

Philip Hasheider, *How to Raise Cattle: Everything You Need to Know,* Motorbooks International, 2007

Ann Larkin Hanson, *Beef Cattle: Keeping a Smale-Scale Herd for Pleasure and Profit,* Bow Tie Press, 2006

Peter King, *Traditional Cattle Breeds and How to Keep Them,* Farming Books and Videos, 2004

Valerie Porter and Sally Seymour, *Caring for Cows,* Whittet Books, 1991

William Rayner Thrower, *The Dexter Cow and Cattle Keeping on a Small Scale,* Faber, 1954

Heather Smith Thomas, *Getting Started with Beef and Dairy Cattle,* Storey Books, 2005

—— *Storey's Guide to Raising Beef Cattle,* Storey Books, 2000

Eddie Straiton, *Calving the Cow and Care of the Calf,* Whittet Books, 2000

—— *Cattle Ailments: Recognition and Treatment,* Whittet Books, 2002

Bill Thicket, Dan Mitchell and Bryan Hallows, *Calf Rearing,* Crowood Press, 2003

Rosamund Young, *The Secret Life of Cows,* Farming Books and Videos, 2005

Alpacas and Llamas

More and more smallholders are getting seduced into keeping alpacas and their larger relatives, llamas. It's easy to see why, first because they are beautiful creatures, with those big doe-like eyes and friendly personalities. You can't really get a more attractive animal, in my opinion. Gerry has so far put his foot down and stopped me venturing into the world of camelids (South American animals which include llamas, alpacas, camels, guanacos and vicuñas), but I hope that one day I'll make him change his mind.

Llamas have a natural instinct to protect their herd. They have been known to protect sheep and even poultry from fox attacks.

Camelids are popular for a variety of reasons; they are long-lived (from twelve to more than twenty years) and make excellent pets, help graze land effectively, and their fleeces produce a fine fibre which can be spun like wool. Llamas, in particular, are strong and easy to train as pack animals, and are often used by rural tourist attractions for trekking or pulling carts. They also have a reputation for protecting sheep and poultry from fox attacks. As camelids are not reared for food, they are not subject to the tagging and movement regulations which apply to farmed animals.

Herd animals by nature, camelids should not be kept alone. You will be hard-pressed to find a reputable breeder who will sell you just one; they should be in groups of two or more, and they are quite happy sharing a paddock with other livestock. Stocking rates recommended by the British Camelids Association are six to eight alpacas per acre (0.5ha) or four to five llamas per acre, though some breeders suggest fewer. As with all livestock, a lot will depend on the nature of your land and what it can cope with.

Alpacas

Alpacas normally command more of an 'aaaahh!' factor than llamas because of their manageable size and tufted heads. They normally reach 1m (39") tall at the shoulder and weigh anything between 45kg and 85kg (99lb to 187lb). There are different types of alpacas, but the kind you are most likely to see is the huacaya, which is probably the most hardy. They come in a wide range of colours, including all shades of brown, black and grey. Less common is the suri, which has a long, soft fleece made up of what look like dreadlocks.

Llamas

Two types of llama are normally seen in the UK: ccara and tampuli. The most common is the ccara, which has a short- to medium-length coat. Llamas are generally cheaper to buy than alpacas, but they are larger and take up more space – an adult llama can be as tall as 115cm (45") and can weigh as much as 160kg (350lb).

Accommodation

A three-sided field shelter or an open barn for shelter from the rain and sun is normally sufficient for both alpacas and llamas, as they are hardier than they look. Normal stock-fencing is usually able to contain them, though some breeders recommend an additional strand of wire on top for llamas – but not barbed wire, as the wool can get caught. Unlike other large animals, alpacas and llamas don't tend to poach the ground, because they have padded feet. Another bonus is that they are very clean and tidy animals, choosing a few specific sites for dropping dung – which makes clearing up after them a lot easier.

Feeding

Alpacas and llamas are described as 'semi-ruminants', and will live on grass throughout the year, though you may need to feed hay, especially if grazing is poor in the winter. As their ancestors came from mountainous regions, they are specially adapted to living on poor-quality food, but some breeders feed a supplement, such as Camelibra, to combat any potential deficiencies. Feeding small amounts of such a concentrate can also help with taming and handling. Alpacas and llamas are natural browsers – like goats, but not as destructive – and enjoy variety in the diet.

Caring for camelids

When compared to other types of domestic livestock, alpacas and llamas need very little done in the way of routine maintenance. They do need to be wormed and vaccinated (against clostridial diseases), and their feet need to be trimmed a few times a year, depending on the type of land on which they are kept. Fortunately, they don't suffer from foot rot, they don't need to have their tails docked and rarely suffer from fly-strike. Alpacas generally need to be sheared once a year (but suris are often every other year), using an electric sheep shears. Llamas can be sheared, but it isn't essential as the fibre can be harvested by combing. Teeth can become overgrown if they don't get sufficient wear, and may need to be trimmed by a vet using equine dental equipment.

FURTHER INFORMATION

British Camelids Association, tel. 01608 661893 (*www.britishcamelids.co.uk*)

British Alpaca Society, tel. 0845 331 2468 (*www.bas-uk.com*)

British Llama Society, tel. 01409 231704 (*www.britishllamasociety.org*)

Alpaca Seller UK, tel. 01730 823256 (*www.alpacaseller.com*)

RECOMMENDED READING

Linda C. Beattie, *Making the Most of Your Llama,* Kopacetic Ink, 1998

Gina Bromage, *Llamas and Alpacas: A Guide to Management,* Crowood Press, 2006

Claire Hoffman and J. Asmus, *Caring for Llamas and Alpacas: A Health and Management Guide,* Rocky Mountain Llama Association, 2000

MAGAZINES

Alpaca World (*www.alpacaworldmagazine.com*)

A Touch of the Exotic

So you think traditional domestic livestock are a bit boring? You fancy rearing something slightly more unusual to create a novel niche market, perhaps? The face of farming in the UK is changing like never before and more and more traditional farmers are looking towards 'exotic' animals as a way of making a living in increasingly difficult times. But however many 'proper' farmers decide to opt for something slightly out of the ordinary, you can guarantee that the majority of those who take the gamble will be smallholders who just fancy trying to make money out of a 'novelty' species.

Rheas are becoming increasingly popular with producers of niche market meats – but many are kept solely as pets.

Alpacas and llamas used to be considered exotic livestock, but they are now becoming common sights in many parts of the UK. Whereas 'livestock' once meant cows, pigs and sheep, there are now farms rearing everything from ostriches and rheas to water buffalo and wild boar. Apart from the standard statutory requirements, some factors to bear in mind are how your neighbours might react to living next door to some exotic beasts, the reliability of your fences and other security measures, and how you might market the meat or other products. Of course, it goes without saying that you should get some experience with conventional livestock under your belt before venturing into anything too ambitious. You've been warned!

Big birds!

Ostriches have been raised in the UK since the late 1980s. There are more than thirty farms raising ostriches in the UK, with the end products being incredibly low-fat meat, as well as feathers, oil and leather. The ostrich may not be able to fly, but it is the world's largest bird, equipped with super-strong legs which can carry it at speeds up to 70km (over 43 miles) per hour. They can reach more than 3m (10ft) tall and weigh more than 180kg (400lb).

Although originally from Africa, ostriches cope well with our climate – but they do need to be provided with shelter from wind and rain and they need a dry sleeping area. The biggest drawback is the security aspect. Ostriches are massive, powerful birds, and are, not surprisingly, among the species listed under the Dangerous Wild Animals Act,

133

1976. This means anyone who wants to keep them must first apply for a Dangerous Wild Animals Licence from the local authority. Emus were recently removed from the list of animals which have to be licensed.

One of the conditions of the Dangerous Wild Animals Licence is that the animals have to be safely contained, so perimeter fencing must be suitable to prevent birds escaping and to prevent intruders or animals getting in. Fencing has to be a minimum of 1.7m (5' 6") high but 2m (6' 6") is recommended for adult birds. Fence posts have to be sunk into concrete or secured in some other way so that they can withstand the impact of an adult bird.

Rheas are ratites, belonging to the same family as ostriches, emus and turkeys, and have a similar appearance, but are much, much smaller. Don't get me wrong, it is still a big bird, standing about 1.5m (5ft) high, but it is about a fifth of the weight of an ostrich, at up to 27kg (60lb). Caring for something that meets you at eye level or below – instead of towering above you – is a lot easier. Generally, socialized rheas are friendly creatures and, accordingly, are not governed by the Dangerous Wild Animals Act.

Rhea meat is growing slowly in popularity, and has the same great selling point as ostrich meat – low fat, low calorie, great taste – but many more people are keeping them as quirky and endearing pets. I think they are absolutely super birds, and wouldn't mind trying to rear some for meat, but I think I'd have a hard job parting with them when it came to slaughter time.

Water buffalo

With their massive horns and powerful bodies, water buffalo look rather fierce and intimidating, but I must admit I've got a real soft spot for them. They are, on the whole, incredibly docile creatures, and much more interesting than conventional cattle. More and more water buffalo are appearing on farms across the UK as demand for their lean meat and low-fat milk increases. I first came into contact with water buffalo through my work with the six Welsh Wildlife Trusts. Water buffalo are becoming an increasingly popular conservation tool, particularly on wetland nature reserves, where conventional livestock aren't appropriate. The Wildlife Trust of South and West Wales was the first to use them, putting them into the Teifi Marshes reserve in Ceredigion, where they do a tremendous job, chomping through tough vegetation like gorse and blackthorn, helping to keep areas of wetlands open for wading birds. Two other Wildlife Trusts in Wales – Montgomeryshire and North Wales – have since followed suit and acquired herds.

I earned my spurs as a buffalo girl when we decided to take a cow and calf to the Royal Welsh Agricultural Show at Llanelwedd, Builth Wells. Part of my work is organizing the Trusts' presence at such events, so looking after the water buffalo for the week suddenly seemed to fit into my job description. Considering we had never met, we got along really well. Even though Star had a 3-month-old calf with her, she didn't mind me clambering into her pen to shovel up another load of muck. Quite the opposite, in fact – she was incredibly curious and eager for attention.

Buffalo milk is low in fat and high in nutrients and can help those with allergies to cows' milk.
The meat is a healthy option too.

Water buffalo cost about the same as conventional cattle, and don't need to be treated any differently. They don't require a Dangerous Wild Animals Licence – just the usual tagging and passports, but they do need really good fencing. The big bonus, for anyone concerned about costly vets' fees (and who isn't?) is that they are relatively low-maintenance creatures, which don't seem to fall prey to the usual bovine ailments. Although milk yield is much less than traditional cattle, what is produced is highly sought after by those with dairy allergies who don't like the taste of goats' milk. Several companies are selling 'niche market' products made from buffalo milk, including yoghurt, ice cream and, of course, cheese. The meat is wonderful, too – lean and tasty, like the best fillet steak.

Wild boar

I've always been fascinated with wild boar and recently got the opportunity to buy my first hybrid wild boar weaners. They are absolutely amazing animals – much more con-fident and more intelligent than normal domestic pigs – and they also have that touch of the exotic about them that makes them a little bit more special.

Pure-bred wild boar are covered by the Dangerous Wild Animals Act 1976, and you must have a licence from the local authority to keep them. Your premises need to be inspected to make sure a whole range of conditions – covering everything from

Wild boar are often crossed with domesticated pigs. These are some of Liz's cross breeds.

housing to security – are satisfied, and you have to have liability insurance in case of break-outs or accidents. Even if just one of the parents is a true wild boar, the same regulations apply. However, with second generation hybrids (and later, like mine), the rules – including tagging and movement regulations – are the same as for domestic pigs.

Crossing a pure bred male wild boar with a domestic pig makes economic sense because female offspring are able to farrow twice a year – unlike their ancestors – and have bigger litters. The drawback, of course, is that the more domestic blood that goes in, the more risk there is of losing the distinctive gamey-flavoured meat, which is so much in demand these days.

One word of warning – wild boar, whether pure or hybrid, will dig for Wales. I've never seen piglets with such an instinct for digging; normally, it takes a few months before my young Tamworths start rooting about, but these little beasts were tearing up the grass from just eight weeks old. Understandably, then, you need good fencing, and you might want to attach a string of barbed wire across the bottom, to try and discourage inquisitive little snouts.

RECOMMENDED READING

Joseph Batty, *Ostrich Farming,* Beech Publishing House, 1998

Laurent Cabanau, *Wild Boar in Europe,* Konemann UK, 2006

D. Charles Deeming, *The Ostrich: Biology, Production and Health,* CABI Publishing, 1999

M. Fahimuddin, *Domestic Water Buffalo,* South Asia Books, 1991

Martin Goulding, *Wild Boar in Britain,* Whittet Books, 2003

Phillip and Maria Minnaar, *The Emu Farmer's Handbook: Commercial Farming Methods for Emus, Ostriches and Rheas,* Hancock House Publishing, 1998

National Research Council, *The Water Buffalo: New Prospects for an Underutilized Animal,* Books for Business, 2002

WEBSITES

www.britishwildboar.org.uk British Wild Boar

www.cgce.net/rea Rhea and Emu Association

www.labellerouge.com The Buffalo Dairy

www.northwalesbuffalo.co.uk North Wales Buffalo

www.ostrich.org.uk British Domesticated Ostrich Association

www.world-ostrich.org World Ostrich Association

GROWING YOUR OWN

I F YOU'RE EXPECTING an Alan Titchmarsh-style 'idiot's guide' to keeping yourself and your household supplied with fruit and veg all year round, you're going to be disappointed. Teaching the basics of gardening is beyond the remit of this book, and there are plenty of books on the market which claim to do just that, so I'm not going to attempt it. In any case, if you've decided to take on a smallholding, chances are you're pretty green-fingered already, and know exactly what you want to grow, why you want to grow it and how to get started. No point in trying to teach you to suck eggs. And they don't taste that good raw, either. This chapter is a short introduction to feeding your livestock off the land. After all, when you're a smallholder, your livestock have to come first. You look after them well, and they'll look after you.

The Green, Green, Grass of Home

One of my old lecturers at the agricultural college used to say that grass was the most important crop of all and, when you think about it, that makes quite a lot of sense. Many non-farmers and newcomers to smallholding alike make the mistake of thinking that grass is a free food for livestock. When you begin managing your grass for livestock, however, you quickly realize that it is not free – because pasture has to be fertilized to help keep it healthy and productive – and it takes a great deal of time to look after, so there is a time cost, too. Pasture management is a year-round job, and skimping on maintenance can have drastic results.

The Controllable and the Uncontrollable

The climate and the altitude of your holding are two things you can do nothing about. A holding plagued by cold and wet weather and situated in a high, exposed position

Table III. Calendar for grassland management

Time of year	Action	Reason
Late winter	Carry out a soil test to establish pH and other nutrient levels.	Optimum soil pH for grass growth is 6 to 6.5. Soil which is too acidic will need an application of lime to correct the pH. Potash, phosphate, and nitrogen are also needed for good growth. Deficiencies may mean a compound fertilizer is needed.
	Clear ditches and check land drains.	Action now saves remedial work later on.
	Plough if reseeding is planned in the spring.	To create drainage channels and ease compaction.
Early spring	Harrow	Harrowing tugs out all the dead grass (or thatch) so that air, water and nutrients get to the soil can more efficiently. This should be carried out in the early spring, before the grass starts to grow in earnest.
	Reseed if necessary (this may be better delayed to late spring in some areas)	To cover bare patches or poorly covered areas.
	Roll if necessary	Rolling will repair damage caused by hooves over the winter. It helps to maximize root contact with available nutrients.
	Apply nitrogen, phosphates or potash fertilizers where necessary (again, may be better delayed to late spring in some areas)	Results of the soil test will have told you whether fertilizers are needed. Timing of the application is crucial; conditions need to be right for nutrient uptake, and to prevent nutrients being washed out of the soil by rain.

(continued)

Time of year	Action	Reason
Late spring/ early summer	If fields are not being grazed sufficiently, cut with a tractor and topper and maintain a length of about 5cm (2–3"). If the land is grazed sufficiently in April, May and June, there may be no need to cut.	At this length, grass can make its own nutrients more efficiently. It is also more resilient against the impact of hooves at this length.
	Target invasive weeds such as dock and poisonous ragwort	Removal early in the year is easier than waiting until they have become established
Summer	Hay- or silage-making time	Grass is about to come into flower. Cut now before it becomes more stemmy and fibrous and less digestible. Cutting and storing now for winter feed means nutrients are retained. Grass which has stopped growing has less nutritional value.
	If not cutting for hay or silage, keep mowing/operating controlled grazing to keep grass length to 5cm	Helps to stop weeds from flowering and setting seed
Mid/late summer	Take a second cut for hay/silage if grass is good enough	Provides more overwinter feed
	Reseed bare patches if necessary	Sometimes conditions are better than reseeding earlier in the year.
Autumn	Keep grazing/mowing.	Autumn grass growth can be vigorous.
	Carry out field maintenance tasks, e.g. repairing fences, laying hedges, etc.	Take the opportunity to work while the weather is still good.
Winter	Keep livestock off wet fields and rotate between other fields as necessary.	Minimizes the risk of poaching and compaction by livestock and allows grass and ground to recover. Sheep need to be kept off wet field to reduce risk of catching fluke. Rotating also reduces risk of foot rot.

Note: This is a rough guide to care and maintenance. Your location, climate and other individual circumstances may alter the time of year you do things, and necessitate additional tasks.

will not have the best grass. Similarly, a steep, sloping field will have shallower soil than one which is bowling-green flat, and it will lose nutrients faster as water drains away.

One thing you can improve, however, is the soil. Maintaining a good, stable soil structure can increase water-holding capacity, and promote root growth. It will also help maintain aeration and drainage, make cultivation easier and reduce the risk of erosion. Well-structured soils are essential for grass and crop growth throughout the year. Compaction, smearing and surface-capping of soils lead to reduced air movement, poor drainage, restricted plant root growth and limited uptake of soil and fertilizer nutrients. This, in turn, means a shorter growing season, reduced stock-carrying capacity, nutrient loss, increased soil erosion and poorer grass growth – but more weeds.

If you're a compete beginner, it really would pay to seek professional advice on what to do with your land and also to get an experienced contractor in to help get the land in shape. Depending on what needs doing, he or she may suggest ploughing to create better drainage and to break through compacted layers; aerating the top soil, using a spiked roller to break the surface and allow the soil to 'breathe' and water to penetrate the soil, so improving root distribution and nutrient uptake; adding lime or organic matter to improve soil stability and encourage earthworm activity; installing and maintaining drains, because wet soils are more prone to damage.

Hay, Silage and Haylage

Feeding livestock over the winter months can be an expensive business, so most farmers choose to keep their costs down by harvesting grasses and cereal crops while they are at their most nutritious and storing them for use when the animals are brought indoors. The main way of doing this is by making hay, silage or haylage. Clover is commonly grown with grass because it is nutritious and works well mixed with grass silage or maize silage. It also helps the nitrogen content of the soil, reducing the need for fertilizer.

Hay is made from grasses and other crops which are cut just as they are coming into flower, and then dried before being baled and stored as overwinter feed. The harvested material is allowed to dry so most of the moisture is removed. Moisture-removal is important for the nutritional quality of the hay, but also for safety; if hay is baled from moist grass, the heat produced can be enough to start a fire.

The difficulty, however, is that the success of haymaking depends hugely on the weather. The traditional way of making hay is to harvest the grass and then leave it to dry in the fields for several days, turning at least every day, before it is baled and stored. Rain can be disastrous, and can ruin a hay crop; mould can develop and toxins form, posing risks to livestock.

The unpredictability of the British weather means that silage has grown in popularity. Silage is a form of conserved grass (or other crop, such as maize) which is made by farmers during the summer months when the grass supply is plentiful and not required for grazing. Grass is cut and left for just a day to wilt (wilting leads to faster fermentation and better-quality silage) and then stored in a silage clamp or pit or baled and wrapped in plastic, which effectively 'pickles' it. If stored in a silage clamp, it is compressed to remove air by driving a tractor back and forth over it. Then it is sealed with plastic and weighted down with old tyres.

Silage is quite moist and livestock usually prefer it to hay; it tastes better and the food value is greater. Silage often forms the bulk of the livestock diet during the winter months. Maize is a popular crop for use as silage because it is nutritious and filling. Run-off from silage is incredibly damaging to the environment, being 200 times polluting than untreated sewage, so make sure any leakage does not go anywhere near water-courses.

Haylage is somewhere in the middle between hay and silage. It is wilted rather than dried, to a dry matter content of 55 per cent to 70 per cent, whereas hay is 85 per cent dry matter. It is baled and wrapped or bagged to exclude air. No moulding occurs in well-made haylage after wrapping and nutrient losses from haylage are less than those lost from hay during drying, so the end product is more nutritious.

Other Fodder Crops

On a small acreage, growing fodder crops can be a bit of a luxury, but you may want to grow at least something to supplement your feed bills. Swedes, turnips and mangolds are traditional choices, but you may have other ideas. Whatever you decide to grow, you need to think about rotating your crops – a practice that goes back to Roman times, so is well tried and tested. Crop rotation is the system of growing a series of different types of crops on the same site – and grazing animals – in consecutive seasons. This way, the build-up of pests and diseases is avoided. Growing in this way also helps improve soil structure – because you are alternating deep- and shallow-rooted crops – and helps prevent soils becoming depleted of soil nutrients, as different crops have different requirements. Crop rotation also means that the ground does not need to lie fallow to regenerate, and can be kept in use with little or no need of artificial fertilizers. It can rest whilst still being productive.

Generations ago, every farm was a mixed farm, rearing livestock and growing cereals. Times have changed considerably and farms tend to be one or the other. Changes in subsidies persuaded many farmers to switch from mixed farming to intensive livestock production, and grass is easier to grow and livestock easier to rear in our largely wet and miserable Welsh climate. Cereals also demand a lot of land and specialist equipment for harvesting and planting – or plenty of money to pay contractors.

10

Selling Your Produce

S O, YOU'VE WORKED OUT what you want to do with your land, what livestock you want to raise, what crops you want to grow. Now then, what are you going to do with all your produce? Of course, your plans could just be limited to providing sufficient meat, fruit, and vegetables to keep your own household happy. But what if you end up with more than you can use? The prime example is eggs. We all start with a few more hens than we actually need, just in case they don't all lay as we'd want them to do. Before you know it, they're all laying and the novelty of having freshly laid eggs for breakfast every single day has worn off.

There are only so many egg-based recipes you can stomach in a week, so you start giving your eggs away. Then word gets around and you start selling them to friends, neighbours, work colleagues. You start to struggle to keep up with demand, so you end up buying in more hens to keep your little cottage industry going. It can just grow and grow.

On the other hand, that might be just what you have in mind. Your dream might include selling direct to customers from your own shop, delivering boxes of seasonal produce by mail order over the internet. Or what about setting up a veg box scheme – or taking a stall at the local farmers' market? There are plenty of options, and it all depends on how much you want to sell, how much time you can devote to marketing and selling, and – very importantly – how much you want to engage with the public.

Local Produce and Growing Demand

Food scares – you name it, we've had it here in the UK. BSE, CJD, salmonella, foot-and-mouth, avian influenza: rightly or wrongly, each crisis or panic wave has made a huge dent in the public's confidence in farm-raised food. As supermarkets bear the brunt of the backlash, smaller, local producers are beginning to reap the benefits. The public's insecurity is fixed on the vast, multinational companies which provide cheap food in ever-increasing quantities. Although there will always be a market for cheaply pro-duced food – much of it from overseas – there is no doubt that the tide is turning in favour of food with integrity.

At one time, cheap meat was all we wanted. But now more and more of us want to know where meat came from, how it was raised and how many miles it travelled before finding its way into our shopping baskets. Celebrity chefs like Jamie Oliver, Gordon Ramsay and Hugh Fearnley-Whittingstall have been great pioneers of local produce, urging TV viewers to buy food grown or reared in their own communities. All good news for smallholders looking for customers.

Research for the National Farmers' Retail and Markets Association (FARMA) has shown that 30 per cent of people in the UK use farmers' markets, but that 92 per cent would do so if more were available. FARMA secretary Rita Exner says the interest in shopping locally is growing fast:

> We reckon the whole sector – farm shops, farmers' markets, pick-your-own, box schemes, and other means of selling direct – is worth about £2bn in the UK alone, which is roughly 2 per cent of the total grocery market. Of that £2bn, £200m is farmers' markets turnover. We think farmers' markets have really struck a chord with people who are wanting more information about the food they are buying and eating.
>
> Being able to meet the people who have produced your food at the market is also a real bonus and it's also a very sociable experience.

Lloyds TSB's regional agricultural manager for Wales, Gwilym Francis, is convinced that 'local' is the new buzz word where food is concerned. Shoppers are now more con-cerned about protecting the environment, using sustainable food sources and cutting back on food miles:

> This is coupled with increasing affluence, which means consumers are more like-ly to seek out niche, speciality foods, and is reflected in the enormous popularity and growth in the number of farmers' markets. Farmers should be able to realise considerably higher prices than for commodity sales – assuming they get their marketing right.

A guide published by Lloyds TSB Agriculture gives a brief and practical overview of the growth of demand for local food, and shows how farmers can connect more directly with consumers and benefit more from selling locally. *The Signpost Guide to Local Food* looks at the opportunities available to farmers, and outlines the ways in which trading on 'localness' can boost farm income. Copies are available from the Lloyds TSB Regional Agricultural Office in Wales on 01267 233614.

Health and Safety and the Sale of Food

The need to understand the rules and regulations governing the preparation, storage, transport, and sale of foodstuffs is paramount. Without wishing to sound alarmist, there is vast scope for disaster when food handling is concerned, and recent high-profile cases involving salmonella, E. coli and other nasties have shown that no one can be too careful. A case of food poisoning not only has the potential to kill your business – it could kill your customers, too.

The Food Standards Agency (FSA) has prepared some excellent documents offering an introduction to the current legislation. These include *FSA Guidance on the Requirements of Food Hygiene Legislation* and *Starting Up: Your First Steps to Running a Catering Business*, which can be downloaded from its website (*www.food.gov.uk*). For more specific information about the type of business you are planning to run, contact your local authority's environmental health department.

All premises used for storing, preparing, distributing or selling food must be registered with the local authority at least twenty-eight days before opening for business. All types of food businesses – shops, market stalls, mobile catering vans, vending machines

Farmers' markets, like this one in Riverside, Cardiff, give customers the chance to meet the producer face to face.

and food delivery vans – are subject to the same regulations, and these regulations apply whether you sell the food publicly or privately, for profit or for fundraising. They do not apply to food cooked at home for private consumption.

Everyone involved in supplying food for sale for human consumption must meet basic hygiene requirements – in all aspects of the business. This covers everything from the premises and facilities used to the personal hygiene of staff. Before you start any food-related venture, talk to the environmental health and trading standards departments in your local authority for advice well in advance. Make sure you understand the legislation, what is required of you as a producer and seller of food, and that you can fulfil all of the requirements.

Common sense will tell you that signing up on a college course which gives you a basic food hygiene certificate is a good idea – and your local environmental health officer may very well insist on it. Most colleges of further education will run such courses. All food businesses must have a Hazard Analysis and Critical Control Points (HACCP) manual. This is a food safety management system which identifies things which might go wrong in your processes, and details the measures you have in place to control or prevent hazards occurring.

All staff in contact with food must receive appropriate supervision, and be instructed and/or trained in food hygiene, to enable them to handle food safely. There is no legal requirement for staff to undergo formal training, nor have relevant qualifications, but many business operators prefer them to do so.

Selling Eggs

You may fancy disposing of your surplus eggs by selling to friends, neighbours and passers-by. The good news is that, if you have fewer than 350 hens, and all the eggs are sold directly to the individual consumers at your farm gate or through door-to-door sales, you do not need to register with the Egg Marketing Inspectorate. The eggs must not be sold graded into sizes.

However, if you have more than fifty hens and you sell some of your eggs at a public market, you be will required to register and you will have to stamp your eggs with a producer identification number which will be issued to you on registration (tel. 01902 693145 or e-mail alistair.blacklock@animalhealth.gsi.gov.uk). If you have fifty hens or fewer, although the eggs do not need to be stamped, you will need to display your name and address on your stall. The food and drink section of DEFRA's website (*www.defra.gov.uk*) has a downloadable document explaining in full the rules governing egg sales.

Remember, also, that if you have fifty birds or more – of any species and at any time of the year – you will need to register your flock with the Great Britain Poultry Register. See the website *poultry.defra.gov.uk* (note no www. prefix) or ring 08459 335577.

Selling at Farmers' Markets

It may seem as if farmers' markets have been around forever, but the concept is a fairly recent import from the USA. In September 1997 Bath became the first city in the country to have a farmers' market as we know it today. It was an instant success and, today, there are more than 550 farmers' markets operating throughout the UK, with more than half being members of FARMA, the organization set up to represent producers selling directly to the public. FARMA certifies farmers' markets in the UK which operate under its guidelines. Certification means they have been independently inspected and meet FARMA standards, ensuring that stallholders are local farmers, growers and food businesses selling their own produce.

Farmers' markets can be run by farmers' co-operatives, local authorities, community groups, or private companies. Regulations vary from one market to another, but most are based on the same kind of criteria:

- Farmers' markets exist to enable local farmers and producers to sell direct to the public; to give consumers the chance to buy fresh, locally grown fruit and vegetables, locally reared meat and home-made products; and to raise public awareness on issues such as genetically modified (GM) foods and the importance of preserving the rural economy.
- Producers must have grown, raised, baked, processed or caught all food sold. The term 'producer' includes the stallholder's family and employees when they are directly involved in the business.
- Stallholders cannot sell products or produce on behalf of, or bought from, any other farm or supplier. This ensures complete traceability.
- Produce must be from a defined 'local' area. 'Local' is usually taken to mean within thirty to fifty miles of the market. However, producers from further afield may be considered if the produce they are selling cannot be sourced within the specified 'local' radius. In the case of applications for pitches by producers of similar foods, preference is normally given to the most local producer.
- The origin of the product, including where it was reared and/or processed, should be on all labelling.
- Stallholders must comply with all local and national laws and regulations regarding the production, labelling, display, storage and sale of goods. All producers must comply with the current food hygiene regulations (see the Food Standards Agency website, *www.food.gov.uk*).
- Organizers will almost certainly ask to see the producer's public and product liability insurance certificate; producers will generally have £5m worth of cover for each. Public liability insurance protects against claims by a third party injured or damaged as a result of your business – for example, if your stall falls down and hurts someone. Product liability insurance protects against claims arising from the actual food you are providing.

- Producers should display trading names clearly on their stalls, together with a contact address.
- By law, prices must be clearly displayed – either on the pack or prominently on the stall. Having to ask for prices is off-putting to customers, and will scare some away.
- Most loose foods (for example, fruit and vegetables) must be sold by net weight, using approved metric weighing equipment. If the food is prepacked, the metric weight must be marked on the pack, but you can also add an imperial weight in a less prominent position. You must have good weighing scales, calibrated for metric weights and approved by your local Trading Standards officer. Spot-checks of your scales can be made at any time either at the market or at your farm.
- Producers 'adding value' to primary local produce (for example, by baking) should use local ingredients wherever possible. Some market organizers specify a minimum percentage of local ingredients to be used.
- Generally, products containing GM products are not permitted to be sold.

The pros

The farmers' market can provide an excellent platform for your wares, allowing you to sell quality food at a good price to an audience which is already convinced about the whole issue of paying a little more for a premium product. Cutting out the middleman means you get the full retail price – sometimes as much as three times the wholesale price.

There can be a great deal of satisfaction to be derived from dealing direct with the public, talking about your produce, your farm and your lifestyle, and collecting feedback from satisfied customers. You don't get that when you hand over your produce to a middleman.

Farm-gate customers may turn up in dribs and drabs, but at farmers' markets customers can come thick and fast, with thousands of potential buyers turning up during the space of just a few hours.

Unlike opening a shop, the start-up costs are low, with the main outlay (aside from the obvious costs involved with producing your food) being the rent of your pitch and getting to and from the site. Another great benefit is that most of your transactions will be in lovely, lovely cash, so there's no hanging around waiting for payment, nor waiting for cheques to clear.

The cons

You have to be incredibly committed. If you do well, your customers will expect to see you there every time (every week or month, depending on how frequently the market is held). It's no good deciding that you'd like next Sunday off; as well as annoying the market organizers, you'll risk disappointing potential customers, who might just go and find someone else to buy from. Remember that, once you've got your pitch, you'll be expected to turn up regardless of the weather. Farmers' markets aren't a fair-weather occupation.

You will have to be willing to put in a phenomenal amount of time and organization into getting your goods ready for sale. Think, for instance, about raising livestock to sell meat at market. You will want to be selling fresh, rather than frozen, so you will have to ensure that your animals will be ready for slaughter when you need them. This means knowing when your animals need to be born or bought in, which can take a bit of working out.

At the other end of the process, you will also have to factor in butchery, processing, packing and labelling time – probably just days before the market. It's going to be a bit of a juggling job, and not one to be taken on without careful consideration and planning.

Oh, and one more thing – what happens if you don't sell everything on market day? What would you do with the leftover food? Customers generally prefer fresh produce, so do you have a Plan B to kick into action if your produce doesn't exactly fly off the trestle table?

Before you Go Any Further

Draw up a business plan. Work out how much profit you will need to make to support yourself and any partner or family, and how much food per week or month you will need first to produce, and second to sell, to achieve your goal. Think about your setting-up costs: product and public liability insurance; buying and running a vehicle to transport your goods; buying or making a stall from which to sell; buying storage facilities, such as a chiller and/or freezer; buying and/or designing packaging and labelling, etc.

Consider whether you really do have the time and commitment. Don't forget that someone has to look after the smallholding while you're preparing for a market or actually selling – and what would happen if you or your partner were to fall sick? Who would take over then?

Talk to the environmental health and Trading Standards departments in your local authority for advice on the latest regulations. Make sure you understand the legislation, what is required of you as a producer and seller of food, and that you can fulfil all of the requirements.

Explore other ways of selling your produce. It may be that farm gate or mail order sales would be less time- and energy-consuming and, potentially, more profitable.

So you Really Want to Take the Plunge?

Here are some basic tips on making sure your stall is a great success and stands out from all the rest:

- Create an attractive and colourful display which will stop browsers in their tracks. Include information and pictures of your livestock, your farm and the food preparation process, and display rosettes you've won for your livestock or produce. Purpose-built, brightly coloured market stalls are available from specialist dealers and often come up for sale on eBay.

- Get to the market in plenty of time to start setting up. Don't just throw your display together, because first impressions are vitally important.
- Make sure all your products are clearly labelled – not just to comply with legislation, but to make life easier for your customers.
- Think about your appearance – smile and be welcoming. Crisp white overalls or colourful aprons always look smart and professional. Tie your hair back or wear a hat, and make sure your hands and nails are clean.
- Talk to your potential customers – engage them in conversation and offer them samples. Tell them about other farmers' markets you attend.
- Offer free samples (just small ones, mind) to stimulate interest. Use the tasting session as an opportunity to engage further with your potential customer – ask them for their views on what they have just tried and tell them more about your foods and how they are produced.
- Don't be afraid of giving special offers like 'buy one, get one free' promotions. But don't undervalue your products. Do your homework beforehand and find out what others supplying similar foods are charging.
- Use the media. Think of new angles to promote your business. Are you, for instance, the first producer to be selling a certain type of food at your farmers' market? Are you using unusual ingredients or a novel way of processing? Has your business won a grant which has allowed you to boost production? Have you taken on new staff? Have you won an award for your produce? Have you won over a celebrity customer with your wares?
- Persevere! You're not necessarily going to be an instant hit at your first market, and it can take quite some time before you start building up regular customers who come and seek you out. However, if you stick at it, hang onto the same stall in the same place and keep providing quality food, chances are you'll start to see the same faces coming back time and time again. The proof of the pudding is when new customers arrive saying friends have recommended your produce. That's the kind of thing that makes all the hard work and commitment worthwhile.

FURTHER INFORMATION

www.farma.org.uk National Farmers' Retail & Markets Association (FARMA)

www.farmersmarkets.net Directory of FARMA-certified farmers' markets in the UK plus advice on setting up and running a farmers' market

www.fmiw.co.uk Farmers' Markets in Wales

www.food.gov.uk Food Standards Agency, for all regulations relating to food preparation and handling

www.food.gov.uk/wales Food Standards Agency Wales Provides information about food-related issues in Wales as well as access to the main FSA site

11

LIVING WITH NATURE

E VER SINCE I STARTED writing my weekly column about smallholding in the *Western Mail*, I've been getting a steady stream of letters and e-mails from readers who want to manage their land, but in a way which benefits wildlife and the environment generally. They may be planning to achieve some degree of self-sufficiency, or they may be setting up small-scale commercial enterprises after 'downshifting' from stressful city jobs. Whatever their plans, they all seem to have one thing in common: they want to do the best they can to give nature a helping hand.

Agriculture has done a phenomenal amount of environmental damage over the decades but now, with increasing awareness of the need to preserve the wildlife and the landscape that still remains, there are signs that times are changing. The reform of the Common Agricultural Policy (see Chapter 6) and the severance of the link between subsidies and production has forced a change in the way landowners operate. The new subsidy system which rewards them for farming in a wildlife-friendly way, alongside the agri-environment schemes, is already having an impact. Some of the birds and mammals which have been disappearing from farmland at an alarming rate over the years are slowly beginning to return. There is still a long way to go, but the signs are good.

Most smallholders have no desire to farm intensively; most will not rely on the holding as their main source of income, and so have the luxury of being able to make space for nature alongside their livestock and any activities they choose to carry out on their land. As a wildlife-friendly smallholder, you may have really great intentions, but getting started in the business or turning your acreage into your own personal nature reserve may be more complicated than you think. You might, for instance, consider that planting hundreds of native, broad-leaved trees in a wide-open field would be a good way to help wildlife. Well, yes it could be, in some situations, but unless you know what you're doing, you could be destroying a species-rich, wildflower meadow which is already a vitally important habitat for a whole host of wildlife. Similarly, hiring

151

a mini-digger and excavating a large pond in a particularly boggy field may seem like a great plan, but not if the field is a prime example of wet grassland – another fast-disappearing farmland habitat.

What it really comes down to is seeking expert help to determine just what habitats you have on your land and finding out what can be done to preserve and enhance them. Organizations like the Wildlife Trusts – there are six in Wales (see below for details), covering the north, the south and west, the three Powys counties, and Gwent – are always happy to give general advice and can sometimes even spare a conservation officer to pop out and take a look at your site. Bear in mind, however, that they are a charity, and resources are limited, so don't pin your hopes on a whole load of free advice. The best thing to do is to become a member of your local trust and get involved. That way you'll get to know the experts and be able to ask all those burning questions.

Some trusts, such as Gwent Wildlife Trust, run special training courses for new landowners, giving an introduction to nature conservation, explaining the need to conserve particular habitats and giving advice on what steps to take. Radnorshire Wildlife Trust, meanwhile, has pioneered a Private Nature Reserves (PNR) scheme for members who are smallholders. The trust has created a network linking up landowners on its patch and providing help and advice with projects aimed at increasing biodiversity. PNR owners receive a regular newsletter, containing land management advice and species profiles and news of special events, including sessions on species identification and habitat management.

Other Wildlife Trusts have also been considering setting up schemes similar to that run by RWT. Conservationists realize the value of having farmers and smallholders 'on their side', so to speak, in the battle to restore biodiversity. It is all very well having nature reserves and other specially protected areas scattered across Wales, but these little oases have limited value in isolation. If 'stepping stones' of similar habitat are not available in the vicinity, sensitive species are simply left stranded and vulnerable on a remote island of habitat, waiting to die. However, if the next-door neighbours are sympathetic landowners who are carefully nurturing suitable habitat, there is a lot more more hope of survival. Your land can play its bit in fighting extinction.

Becoming a Conservation Volunteer

The best way to learn how to help nature is by getting involved with the work of one of the many organizations concerned with protecting and improving the environment – the Wildlife Trusts, the Woodland Trust, the British Trust for Conservation Volunteers (BTCV), the National Trust, the RSPB, etc. Most bodies in the conservation sector rely heavily on volunteers to carry out essential maintenance work on nature reserves, so you'll normally get the chance to learn traditional countryside management skills like hedgelaying and drystone walling as well as other useful techniques, which might include using a chainsaw and felling trees.

Each local authority has adopted a Local Biodiversity Action Plan (LBAP) which sets out its plans for protecting and improving priority species and habitats. Your local biodiversity officer will be able to give you information on conservation projects taking place in your area which you may be able to get involved with, and offer advice on how to care for specific types of habitat on your land. He or she will also be able to tell you whether any local authority biodiversity grants are available for carrying out conservation work on your holding (see Chapter 6 for more on this). You can find details of how to contact your biodiversity officer on the Wales Biodiversity Partnership website (*www.biodiversitywales.org.uk*) under the section 'Local to You', or by ringing your local authority.

Denmark Farm: a Conservation Success Story

Neil and Barbara Taylor wanted to do the best they could for nature when they moved to Denmark Farm, a 40-acre smallholding near Betws Bledrws, Lampeter, west Wales. The site had been farmed intensively in previous years: its commercial rye grass fields and bare hedges were typical of vast areas of grazing land, and the place was almost totally devoid of wildlife. In 1987 they set up the Shared Earth Trust – now a well-respected conservation charity – with the aim of seeing whether the damage caused could be reversed without huge expense. Traditional grazing regimes were reintroduced, and over-grazed areas fenced off to allow nature to regain control; drainage was removed to allow wetland areas to return, and fertilizer use was abandoned.

Even the experts had to agree that the results were pretty amazing. In just a few years, the number of nesting bird species rose from fifteen to forty-six. Fields which had previously been full of rye grass and little else were soon rich in wildflowers, grasses and sedges, with the most diverse meadow containing well over 100 plant species. Small mammals have returned, and fourteen species of breeding dragonfly and damselfly have been recorded on site.

Now a nationally recognized demonstration farm and conservation site, Denmark Farm has built up a reputation as a training centre for landowners looking to give something back to nature. The Shared Earth Trust runs workshops and short courses designed specifically for landowners keen to manage some or all of what they own in a more caring manner. Size doesn't matter: anyone with a patch of land is welcome. Students can learn how to create a conservation plan, restore biodiversity to farmland, plan a pond or develop skills like hedgelaying and coppicing. Find out about courses by ringing 01570 493358 for a booklet, or by visiting the website (*www.shared-earth-trust.org.uk*).

Some Starting Points for Wildlife-Friendly Farming

- Get yourself some professional advice on caring for your land. Don't do anything major until you know what wildlife and habitats you have, and how to deal with them. You need to be sure you aren't destroying an ancient valuable habitat before you plant any trees. Don't fertilize old meadows nor drain wet grasslands.

- Try to provide a variety of habitats – for example, wetlands, old grasslands, heath and woodland – and try to maintain a good mix of crops and livestock. The habitats your land will support will depend on the ground condition and other factors, so be realistic about what can be created.

- Try to minimize the use of fertilizers, pesticides, and herbicides. Keep chemicals and manure away from watercourses. Organic farming, with no application of chemical fertilizers, is usually best for wildlife. If you are going organic, take advice before reseeding pastures, to ensure you are not damaging ancient flower-rich grasslands.

- Use traditional management methods. Grazing is the best way of managing your land – preferably using both cattle and sheep, as they graze in different ways. If grazing isn't possible, cutting is the next best option.

- If you already have fields of wildlife-poor grassland which has been intensively managed, consider whether you want to set off on the long course of restoring it to species-richness. Specialist advice is essential. Fertilizing needs to stop, and the land needs cutting or grazing regularly to help reduce the artificially high fertility in the soil. Wildflower species may return on their own as fertility decreases, or wildflower seed can be sown.

- If you need to keep your improved grassland as productive as possible to support livestock, there are still things you can do to help wildlife. Leave field margins or corners unfertilized and ungrazed/uncut to produce a fringe of rough areas around your more productive grassland. This will help support a greater diversity of plants, more invertebrates, small mammals and their predators.

- Allow rough growth alongside streams and rivers to protect wildlife from run-off from things like fertilizer and pesticides. Any developing thick scrub, or holes around the roots of secluded stream-side trees, could even provide a resting-up place for a passing otter.

- Maintain links between habitats by looking after your hedges and allowing grassy margins to flourish. Don't be too tidy, because overgrown areas give food and shelter.

- Allow stubbles to remain over winter, as they provide a useful source of food for many birds and small mammals. Delay any spraying with pesticides until as near to cultivation as possible.

- Don't remove ivy from walls and mature trees, as it is a source of nectar and fruit for insects and birds late in the year when other food sources are scarce. It is also useful for roosting and nesting birds and hibernating mammals.

▦ If you have any really old trees, look after them, as they can be home to many types of wildlife. Leave standing and fallen dead trees to provide habitat for fungi, insects and birds.

▦ Make sure that bats, and birds like barn owls, swallows, swifts and house martins, can get access to your farm buildings – old and newly built. Put up nest boxes where you can.

▦ Don't lay or cut all your hedges every year, because bushy hedgerows are a rich source of food and nesting material for birds and mammals. When planting new hedges, always use a mix of native and – if possible – locally grown trees and shrubs.

▦ If you have existing ponds, look after them. Take professional advice before making any new ponds, because it might not be the best course of action to help wildlife.

▦ Keep any areas of wet grassland and marshy areas to help waders and wetland plants.

FURTHER INFORMATION

Brecknock Wildlife Trust, tel. 01874 625708 (*www.brecknockwildlifetrust.org.uk*)

BTCV Cymru, tel. 029 2052 0990 (*www.btcvcymru.org*)

Coed Cymru (The Woodland Trust in Wales), tel. 01686 650 777 (*www.coedcymru.org.uk*)

The Countryside Council for Wales, tel. 0845 1306229 (*www.ccw.gov.uk*)

Environment Agency Wales, tel. 08708 506 506 (*www.environment-agency.gov.uk/regions/wales/*)

Forestry Commission Wales, tel. 0845 604 0845 (*www.forestry.gov.uk/wales*)

FWAG Cymru (an independent and provider of environmental and conservation advice and consultancy to farmers), tel. 01341 421456 (*www.fwag.org.uk*)

Gwent Wildlife Trust, tel. 01600 740600 (*www.gwentwildlife.org*)

Montgomeryshire Wildlife Trust, tel. 01938 555654 (*www.montwt.co.uk*)

The National Trust, tel. 01492 860123 (*www.nationaltrust.org.uk*)

North Wales Wildlife Trust, tel. 01248 351541 (*www.wildlifetrust.org.uk/northwales*)

PONT (Pori, Natur a Threftadaeth – Grazing, Nature, and Heritage), the grazing animals initiative for Wales, linking landowners who have land in need of grazing for conservation purposes with livestock owners in search of land, tel. 01874 610100 (*www.grazinganimalsproject.org.uk* e-mail *pont@grazinganimalsproject.org.uk*)

Radnorshire Wildlife Trust, tel. 01597 823298 (*www.radnorshirewildlifetrust.org.uk*)

Wales Biodiversity Partnership (*www.biodiversitywales.org.uk*)

Wildlife Trust of South and West Wales, tel. 01656 724100 (*www.welshwildlife.org*)

Wildlife Trusts Wales, tel. 029 20480070 (*www.wildlifetrustswales.org*)

A YEAR ON A SMALLHOLDING

Many readers of my work in the Western Mail *have suggested I bring out a book featuring the weekly columns I've been writing every Tuesday for the past six years. I haven't got round to doing it yet, but I thought I might include just a few examples in this, my first book, for the benefit – or otherwise – of the uninitiated.*

The columns are very much a kind of diary of some of the disasters and delights my husband Gerry and I have encountered along the way. If you think you could survive a year like this, you're well on your way to being smallholder material!

January

It wasn't a good start to the week. When I opened up the e-mail from the lovely woman who bought our dishwasher, my blood ran cold. You know how it is when you sell something mechanical or electrical. You're always left with that niggling thought in the back of your mind: what if they get it home and it doesn't work?

I had no reason to suspect anything was wrong, of course. It was less than 2 years old and had served us well all the time we'd had it. The only problem we faced when we moved house was that the kitchen just wasn't ready for it. So we stored it out it in the shed, where it was nice and dry, with plans to eventually install it once our renovations were complete. Eventually, however, after a series of hold-ups and changes of plan, we decided to buy one that fitted inside a kitchen cupboard, out of sight.

We gave the old one a good wipe over, to shake off the dust, and it looked good as new. The couple who came to collect it were really pleased with their bargain, too – a fairly new machine at a fraction of the price – and we were glad to have the space in the shed which, like most people's, was crammed so tightly with stuff, we could barely set a foot inside.

Apart from feeling rather guilty that I couldn't find the instruction manual – lost under piles of temporarily relocated kitchen items – I thought nothing more of it. Until that e-mail arrived.

The note from the woman was friendly and chatty, as previous ones had been, but the dreaded line was there: *'To cut a long story short we could not get it to work – lots of noise, no water.'* My heart sank. It got worse. They had to call out an engineer. He, too, was baffled, until he opened up the machine and found … a huge mouse nest, stuffed with straw, chewed-up egg boxes and a store of mixed corn!

Vital wires had been chewed through, too – no wonder it wouldn't work. Needless to say, I was mortified. I read the horror story with my hands clamped tightly to my face, just like that Edvard Munch painting.

This sweet couple had turned up in good faith to buy a dishwasher to make their lives easier now they had a newly born baby to look after – and I had sold them one that couldn't do the job.

To make matters worse, I had sold them something with rodent-ravaged insides – can you imagine what they must have thought? The only comforting thing I could think was thank God no mice had gone with it! I'm still torturing myself with 'what if?' visions. What if, for instance, some mice had stowed away? Chewed electrics, droppings over toys in the nursery … It would be all my fault.

All I could do was apologize profusely and offer send a cheque in the next post. Amazingly, they were really nice about it all, and appreciated there was no way I could have known what was going on inside the innocent-looking white box. In fact, they said they laughed when they made their discovery – because they had been so stumped trying to work out what had gone wrong.

Gerry and I have now got to the stage where we can laugh about it, too – at last. When we delved inside the shed – a Pandora's box of forgotten household items, gardening tools, flower bulbs, plastic decoy birds and car cleaning accessories – we found the tell-tale signs of mouse activity. Feed bags had been nibbled, egg boxes had been chewed into fine, soft bedding, and the floor was peppered with tiny black droppings.

I think a good clean-out is called for this weekend. It'll be a good opportunity to throw out anything we don't need – mice included. And if anything, it's taught us a lesson: if we're offering anything for sale in future, we'll be giving it a damned good shake, just in case!

February

Every smallholder needs a barn. Somewhere to store all those bits and pieces you never thought you'd need until you took the plunge and opted to live in the country. We've had our barn for the best part of a year, now. Not standing and functional, though – lying under a tarpaulin in the carpark in a thousand different pieces, waiting to be put up.

Ever since we moved here, one of the biggest and most costly things on our 'to do' list was getting ourselves some decent storage. Too excited by the prospect of owning a farmhouse and some land, we overlooked the fact that it didn't come with outbuildings. At the time, we didn't think we'd need too much storage space. We thought a few decent-sized sheds would suffice. Wrong.

We already had a tractor mower, a big petrol lawnmower and enough tools, gadgets and gizmos to rival our local B&Q. Soon after we moved, we started acquiring more tools that would help us get the land into the shape we wanted. Before long, we had bought a tractor and topper, an industrial-strength brushcutter, a petrol generator, a chainsaw, a rotavator, a mini-digger and a whole host of tools like slashers, billhooks, log-splitters, scythes, and all those other 'useful' bits and pieces that I couldn't, for the life of me, put a name to.

We had three sheds, full to bursting, a pantry which was anything but what it was intended for, and a boiler house which not only contained the boiler (surprise, surprise), but a whole load of tools.

Then I spotted a bargain on eBay – a galvanized barn in kit form, several thousands of pounds cheaper than the ones we had been looking at. But work – the kind that pays the bills, I mean – got in the way. It's difficult when you're juggling jobs and DIY, and sometimes you just have to bite the bullet and give in. Sometimes it pays to call in the professionals.

Have you ever seen that Harrison Ford film, *Witness*? Ford plays a detective who goes into hiding in an Amish community, and initially finds it a struggle adjusting to their strict ways. Great film, for lots of reasons, but the scene I always remember is the one where Ford joins the rest of the village as everyone turns out to raise a barn from scratch in a day.

Somehow I imagined that when we built our barn, it would be something like that – loads of friends and neighbours turning up to help, children playing in the sunshine in the fields, home-made food and drink ready and waiting to feed the hungry workers. The reality was Gerry and me lugging the metal girders and panels over to the site in the rain, the builder and his sons bolting everything together, and our dogs getting in the way at every possible opportunity.

But at least it was happening at last. It was a bit of a jigsaw job – rather like a giant Meccano set – but the chap we bought the kit from had supplied all the original plans and had helpfully numbered and coded each and every piece. By the end of the first day, the skeleton structure stood tall and impressive – even if it did look a little like a discount carpet warehouse waiting for a McDonalds to be built alongside.

All appeared well until the next morning. Unexpected high winds overnight managed to almost flatten the lot like a pack of cards. It was just like someone had given everything a good shove from the right-hand side, so that the whole, massive structure was leaning precariously to the left. I screamed when I saw what had happened. Gerry, who had gone to work in the dark and hadn't noticed, was speechless when I phoned him with the news. When the builder arrived, his face was an absolute picture, and I only wish I'd had a camera.

Within an hour, however, the whole structure was safely back in place and secured. Miraculously, none of the girders had been damaged.

A few more days' work and we'll hopefully have the cladding on. The barn will be well and truly raised. Fantastic. All I need now is for Harrison Ford to turn up and my dream will be complete.

March

'So, what did you get up to at the weekend?', they asked at work. To be fair, they would never have guessed, so I had to tell them.

'Well, I caught a ram, turned him on his back, clipped his hooves, and then felt him all over to see if he was ready to go for slaughter.' A real conversation stopper, if ever there was one.

I must admit, over the past week or so I've become a bit of an agri anorak. I've started my course for smallholders at Pencoed College, you see, and I'm having such a fascinating time, I seize every opportunity to bore everyone with the details.

There are about a dozen in the class, some with smallholdings, some planning to buy soon, and they come from all walks of life. What we all seem to have in common is the desire to have some control over what we eat, to rear livestock with care and respect, and to eventually make a little bit of money out of running a smallholding if we possibly can. Our twice-weekly, 12-week course promised to give a good overview of the whole business of running a holding or a small farm, with an emphasis on hands-on experience. So far it hasn't disappointed us. The first topic on the list, as you will have gathered, was sheep.

Now I had never been anywhere near a sheep in my life. The closest I got was watching someone bottle-feeding a tiny lamb on a school trip to Folly Farm.

The sheep we saw at Pencoed were huge by comparison. They were barely a year old, but they looked pretty full-grown to me. Back in the class we had learned all about the different breeds, which were best-suited to upland and lowland areas, and how to condition-score an animal to assess its growth and overall progress.

It all seemed fine in theory. But when we left the warmth and security of the classroom and approached the flock of Lleyn ram lambs, I did wonder what I had let myself in for. I decided to apply the 'jumping out of an aeroplane' technique that I often use when I know I have to do something I'm not too sure about; I took a deep breath and got on with it. 'Just get in there and grab one,' said David, our affable tutor. Easier said than done. It was all very well grabbing the fleece around the neck, but for an inexperienced wimp like me, holding on to the frightened beast using all his weight to try and get away was a bit like wrestling with a buffalo.

Then, of course, there was the small matter of flipping him onto his back. I lost count of how many attempts it took, but the sheer satisfaction of finally getting him there was worth all the hard work. Once his shoulders were clamped firmly between my legs, he was powerless. It was weird to see how an animal which could be so powerful on all fours could be rendered helpless once on his back – a bit of a design fault, I thought.

Once the reluctant ram was under my control, he was ready for his pedicure. First all the muck had to be cleaned out from between the cleats, the foot checked for problems like foot rot, and then any uneven bits trimmed off. I was a bit worried about the risk of cutting the cuticle and drawing blood, but once I was into the swing of it, it wasn't too difficult. The only tricky bit was clenching my aching thighs tight enough to keep my patient from wriggling free.

The final task of the day was checking the young ram over to see how much meat was on him, starting by feeling the thickness of the flesh on the hind legs and the prominence of the spine and the knuckle bone in the lower back – to see how well-covered they were at the 'lamb chops end' of the body. So far so good.

'Now put your hand under his tail and see what you can feel,' said David. We all looked at each other.

It had to be done, and there's a first time for everything, I suppose. A strange way to spend Saturday morning, I know. But at least, when I got back to work, I had something to talk about.

April

Not for the first time, living what they laughingly call 'the good life' has taken its toll on me. My joints ache and my muscles have seized up; my arms feel like I've been in a weightlifting competition, and my legs feel like I've run a marathon. There's no official clinical condition to describe this sorry state, but I've borrowed one from the medical journals: trench fever. Yes, I know that the phrase is usually used to to describe the nasty blood-borne infection, first identified in troops serving in the trenches during WWI, but I've decided to adopt it because the cause of all my aches and pains was a trench. Gerry's trench. A really long, deep trench that is taking hours and hours of back-breaking work to fill.

Since he's had a digger to play with, there has been no stopping him. Giving a man a Bobcat is a bit like giving a child a bucket and spade at the seaside: it becomes an obsession. His latest piece of handiwork is this seemingly never-ending trench. He's preparing footings for a big storage shed, you see, so that we can get all our bits of machinery, building materials, and other odds and ends, under one roof.

The only snag is that all our land slopes down away from us, so creating a flat base inevitably means building a substantial retaining wall on three sides, to hold back tonnes of earth. The walls have to sit on concrete footings but, to save money and ma-terials, the bottom half of the trench is filled with rocks and rubble and then topped with concrete. As with all our projects, Gerry and his precious laser level take care of the technical side of things and I provide supplementary labour. I'm no good at drawing plans or working out load-bearing weights or anything essential to a project, but I am good at things that don't require too much brain-power – like moving concrete blocks and shifting stone. No surprise, then, that all I've been doing for the past few days is heaving rocks from A to B. Hence the pathetic physical condition I'm in now.

I should be used to it, of course. This is the second home we've had where hard labour has been required to achieve our aims. In our last place – a modern, split-level house – we built a massive retaining wall to level the back garden, excavated two ponds by hand, and shifted countless tonnes of earth using only shovels and barrows because there was no access for a mechanical digger. Maybe that's why Gerry fell in love with mini-diggers – he's still haunted by the memory of all that manual work. I must admit, he's learned to handle one really well, after several years of practice and just a few minor mishaps along the way. Of course, no one should just go out and hire a digger without knowing how it works and what skills are required to use it safely and efficiently. Even though Gerry is extremely competent now (we won't mention the times when he got stuck in the mud, or when, with the door open, he spun round 360 degrees and wrenched the door off its hinges), he still feels he would benefit from some profession-al training.

In the mean time, the digging and the trench-filling goes on. When the weather is dry, we try and fit a few hours here and there around work, and we're not doing too badly. It still hurts, though. What we both really need at the end of the day is a good, long, soak in a hot bath. Sadly, though, the ageing copper hot-water tank decided to spring an unsealable leak last week so, along with mopping up the dining room below it, we had to drain the system. We've bought a new, state-of-the-art (i.e. expensive) hot-water tank that promises to do all kinds of things. At the moment, however, it's sitting in the bedroom like a big white Dalek, waiting for the plumber to turn up. Cold baths just don't seem that appealing at the moment, so we're both doing without. So just a word of warning – if you do happen to pay us a visit, don't come too close.

May

Fergus and I have been together for quite a few years now, and I never imagined the time would come when we would be going our separate ways.

We've travelled everywhere together in pursuit of pleasure and excitement – high up in the mountains and out to the remotest reaches of the countryside, down secluded muddy lanes and along sandy seashores. We've also been to less thrilling places together, carrying out essential jobs – trips to the abattoir, farmers' markets, the feed merchant's place, and the vet – but each journey has been an adventure, all the same.

Gerry, it must be said, has been very understanding. He appreciates that I need a cer-tain little something extra in my life, and long ago resigned himself to the fact that Fergus and I had something special.

Liz and her trusty Land Rover Fergus have had years of thrilling times together.

Still, nothing is forever, they say, and, after five years together, I've come to realize that my days with Fergus are numbered. Age takes its toll on everyone; his body isn't quite as sleek and trim as it used to be, and he can't do things as fast as he used to, nor for as long. Sometimes he's a little slow to get going and needs some kind words and gentle encouragement.

He always gets there in the end, though, and never really disappoints. The problem is that he's been pretty high-maintenance over the past year and, much as I regret it, I've decided to replace him. I've gone and bought a brand new pick-up truck – all sleek and shiny, with chrome bits, leather seats, air conditioning, carpets, a radio that actually works, and doors that don't fling open when I'm driving down the motorway.

I picked up the new object of my affections last Wednesday and we're getting along fine. It was lust at first sight – great body, good looks, five seats and enough space in the back for a whole host of useful things. This was supplemented by the fact that there were just nine miles on the clock, as it had barely been out of the showroom, and it came with a three-year warranty and lots of other incentives. So it's goodbye to all those trips to the garage every couple of months, and no more astronomical bills for spare parts and major surgery – at least for a while.

To be honest, I think we've probably renewed all the bits that needed renewing by now, so whoever buys Fergus could have many years of trouble-free motoring ahead. He had a lifesaving transplant a few years ago – a 300 TDI engine which goes like a whippet compared to the one that came out – and he certainly has a lot of miles left in him. I've loved being a Landy girl, and it's going to be strange not having one around.

As well as being a faithful companion, a rugged head-turner, and a real conversation-starter, Fergus is incredibly hard-working and also accommodating. He will quite happily pull a trailer with a three-tonne digger on board, and has transported a motley collection of livestock in the back – dogs, pigs, lambs, and even turkeys.

In future, small numbers of animals which don't warrant hitching up the livestock box will be transported in the load bay of the pick-up – thankfully relieving the problem of having to hold your breath when driving. I need to get a hard top and a load liner first, and then Fergus will be put up for sale.

As the time for advertising Fergus draws nearer, I'm starting to get a few guilt pangs about replacing him with a younger model. I took one of the dogs to agility at the weekend; as usual, I used Fergus, because there is no way dogs are going on the back seats of my smart new truck.

As I got in and settled myself in that familiar driving position, I felt comfortable, at ease, and happy; I knew where everything was, and how everything worked. The new truck – as yet unnamed – is still like a new boyfriend on the first date: I'm still feeling my way around, fumbling a bit, and finding out slowly just what he's capable of. I can tell it's going to be another great adventure.

June

This year is flying past already. It doesn't seem that long ago that we were wrapping up against the cold and counting our blessings that we'd ordered plenty of oil for the Aga and the central heating boiler.

All of a sudden, it was like someone flicked a switch and turned on the hottest weather of the year. We're now racing towards the end of June, and already we're being forced to think about the winter.

Take last week, for example. The thermometer on the wall said 40°C, the dogs were lying in the stream, trying to cool down, and all the other animals here looked as though they were wishing they could do the same. In the greenhouse, my precious veg seedlings had been frazzled, necessitating some hasty replanting, and the water in the garden pond had fallen to half its normal level. Everywhere the ground – soaked just a few weeks ago by torrential rain – is parched and cracked, reminiscent of a lunar landscape.

And then the phone rang. It was the woman from the company that supplies our turkeys. 'Just wondering how many Christmas turkeys you'll be ordering this year.' Christmas? Spare me, please!

But that's the trouble with being a smallholder: it's one never-ending cycle of forward planning. The bronze turkey poults, for instance, normally arrive at the end of July. They get here as day-olds, and go under infra-red heat lamps until they're fully feathered and able to survive outdoors. There aren't that many suppliers of good quality poults around, so you have to order early or face disappointment.

I'll never fail to be amazed at how quickly time goes. Looking at the calendar today, I realized it's only two or three weeks until our latest pigs go off to the abattoir. They're looking really good – a bit leaner than the last ones were at this age, because I've resisted the temptation to feed them as much this time. Their successors will arrive in July, ensuring we have plenty of pork in time for Christmas.

The lambs, too, are growing incredibly fast. The ram lamb will be sent for slaughter in the autumn, and the others kept to breed from, along with their mothers. Born in March, they're just about ready for weaning now, so from next week we'll separate them from their mothers and prepare for the deafening howls which will inevitably follow.

Penning the ewes off will, however, give us a good chance to give a top-to-toe examination, trimming the feet, checking the mouths and worming them. Once the old girls are free of their lambs, we can start getting them into condition for breeding again, and making inquiries with local farmers about putting them to a ram.

At about the same time, we'll be hoping to get the goats into kid, too. This autumn is going to be another great voyage of discovery, I'm sure. There's never a dull moment when you're a smallholder – and never much time to sit back twiddling your thumbs, either.

July

Normally I'm pretty good at coping with the *ych a fi** kind of jobs. I've got a pretty strong stomach, and I'll happily (well, maybe not happily) clean pus out of a wound, clear up poo and vomit, or put my hand up a sheep to pull out a lamb, and then clear up the afterbirth.

For a girl brought up in a terraced house in Merthyr, in a family with no connections to farming, I don't think that's too bad. I pride myself on having an attitude that says, if you can wash it off afterwards, don't worry about touching it.

But we all have our weaknesses. Mine is maggots. I simply can't bear the sight or even the thought of them. While others can laugh hysterically at those reality TV programmes which show maggots being poured over people's heads, or blindfolded gameshow contestants forced to put their hands into wriggling masses of the vile little creatures, I'm hiding behind the sofa.

But sometime in our lives, we all have to confront our demons – and I've just done it.

I was cooking a nice beef roast for dinner the other night and thought I'd take a stroll down to see the lambs while it was finishing off. All was well until I saw Dotty, my favourite sheep, stretching her neck round, trying to reach her side with her head. Alarm bells started ringing. Fly-strike. Bad weather and other complications had meant that the sheep weren't sheared as early as I'd have liked this year and, despite having been doused with stuff to keep the flies away, it looked like they had already laid their eggs and the young had hatched out.

It took a few seconds before I found the first culprits, hidden deep in her fleece. I knew, of course, that it was going to be much worse than just a few. I summoned help – Josh and Gerry – and between us we began the painstaking process of hand-clipping the immensely thick Suffolk-Texel cross fleece. I'll spare you the details of what we found beneath it. Honestly, you wouldn't thank me for telling you. What I will say is that I've never felt so ill in my life, and I still can't believe that I managed to do what I did. Needs must when the devil drives, and all that. It's surprising what we're capable of when we have no choice.

Still, if I felt bad, how about poor old Dotty? She was being attacked in seven different spots, and couldn't do a thing about it.

With the bulk of her fleece gone, and the majority of the disgusting invaders removed, she at least had some relief. It took the three of us almost three hours, mind you. It was gone 10 p.m. and almost dark when we got back to the house. Not surprisingly, no one felt like dinner.

Next morning, I made an SOS call to Mark Powell, a farmer from Aberdare who I first met at the Royal Welsh. I'd been told Mark was a good shearer, and it only took him about ten minutes to do all eight sheep. Sheep seem to know when they're in an experienced pair of hands. Each time he caught and turned a ewe, she would just lie there, like he had hypnotized her. Whenever I try and hold one, there are legs thrashing about everywhere.

I really admire people who can shear confidently and quickly. Last year, I went on a shearing course run by the Wool Marketing Board and, despite expert tuition and constant encouragement, I was really worried about going too close with the clippers, so my fleeces ended up in millions of pieces. What's more, the effort involved nearly killed me. Every bit of my body ached – arms, shoulders, thighs, and bottom – and all over my upper body was black and blue from being kicked by impatient sheep. I swore then that I'd get someone in to do it for me this year, and I'm so glad that they've finally been done.

I've not had much luck with sheep this year – difficult births, stillborn lambs, a prolapse, a death, and now maggot hell. Hopefully, I've seen the worst side of sheep-keeping now, and it should get easier. Experiences like this teach you to be more vigilant, and never to trust to luck. If anyone tells you keeping sheep looks easy, don't believe it.

*Welsh expression of disgust, normally used to describe something really vile or distasteful.

August

One of the really great features of Welsh Mountain Dogs is that they don't chase or kill things. The Bernese Mountain Dog and Newfoundland in their ancestry brings out the big softy in them, making them loving and loyal companions, while the collie part contributes intelligence to the mix, but not the manic herding instinct.

Of course, breeding alone doesn't make the perfect dog, and I've made sure that mine have been introduced to our livestock as early as possible and taught how to behave around other animals. I've never had any problems leaving them alone with poultry, pigs, sheep, or goats, and I know other smallholders who say exactly the same.

Understandably, then, I was horrified and panic-stricken at what confronted me the other day: Gordon, our newest arrival, had blood on his face and a severed turkey head in his mouth.

The 6-month-old pup was clearly as proud as punch, trotting around with his precious trophy and then teasingly turning round and taking it away again, a long gooey red string dangling from it like a pendulum.

My thoughts immediately turned to the Death Shed – the place where I quarantine sick and injured birds while they make up their minds whether to recuperate or expire. Two days earlier, one of the bronze turkeys had hurt its leg and wasn't feeding well because it couldn't summon up the effort involved. Sometimes they do silly things as they try to roost, and end up landing awkwardly. We get one or two casualties every year, and most of the time they recover.

Gordon, like the elder dogs, had been coming with me on my feeding rounds every day, and had given the turkey the odd sniff, but nothing more. I'd had no reason to worry – until now. I had left the shed door open. Curiosity must have got the better of

Liz's young dog Gordon (right) was wrongly accused of a heinous crime.

him and, well, unsupervised puppies will be puppies. All the same, I was bitterly disappointed and faced with a dilemma: how could I nip this in the bud and prevent it from becoming a habit?

Too much to think about right now. First job on the list was to clear away the carnage in the Death Shed. Four steps away from the open door, I heard the unmistakable, high-pitched 'Ow, ow, ow!' of a turkey hen – the turkey hen with the bad leg.

Then it suddenly came to me like a bolt out of the blue: Gordon was innocent. A few days earlier, Gerry had killed a turkey for dinner and had deposited all the nasty bits in an old feed bag, which Gordon's endless appetite and keen sense of smell had tracked down. I knew how Llewelyn must have felt when he realized he had wrongly condemned his faithful dog Gelert to death, thinking it had killed his baby son.

I felt really guilty for thinking so badly of him. I had yelled and yelled until he had dropped his slimy, fleshy plaything and then sent him off to lie in his bed with orders not to move a muscle. OK, so I hadn't drawn a sword and slaughtered him, but I still felt pretty bad.

We're now friends again. In fairness to Gordon, he's turning into a lovely dog; temperament-wise he's got the makings of another Bryn, but his massive feet and strong, broad body suggest he's going to be much bigger. Everyone who meets him is instantly charmed by his happy personality and laid-back attitude, and he gets no end of attention. He's got one unpleasant experience coming up, however: he's getting castrated before Christmas. The other dogs have both been done, and we can't have any youthful testosterone upsetting the order of our cosy little pack, so it has to happen. Once again, I'll be wracked with guilt, but I'm sure I'll get over it.

September

Don't say I told you, but my husband's got this mole. He's hugely embarrassed about others seeing it, worries about it night and day, and he's tried everything to get rid of it. It's a fairly recent affliction – he didn't have it in the last place we lived. But, within months of moving, the tell-tale signs started. Some people may see it as a simple cosmetic problem, but to him it's a hideous scar on an otherwise perfect canvas.

If only *Talpa europaea* could be removed as simply as the other kind of mole that brings misery to people's lives! Perhaps then we'd get some sleep at night. At the moment, I'm observing a battle of wills. The first thing poor Gerry does in the morning is look out of the bedroom window to see if there are any more of those tell-tale volcano-style mounds scarring the fields below. If he spots one, he goes wild, pulling on his clothes, racing down to the offending brown humps, and to stamping them down like a man possessed.

Last week we had a few days away, shopping in France. I thought he might be able to relax for a while, but no. Instead of hitting the hypermarkets to stock up on gallons of cheap wine to relieve the misery of the long, dark, wet, winter days ahead, we went straight to the DIY store Leroy Merlin. It's become a bit of a favourite in recent years, ever since we discovered it was like B&Q for smallholders. Most of the French DIY stores are pretty much the same – they not only have all the usual stuff you'd expect to find, but also a vast range of country management tools, gates, fencing, and so many other useful things – and all much, much cheaper than at home.

We bought our ride-on mower there and saved several hundred pounds in the process. This time we bought some bargain loppers and a really clever log-splitting device that we'd never have found in this country.

Gerry, however, was most keen to check out their pest control section. Much as we love the French, they don't seem willing to tolerate anything which causes them the slightest annoyance, which means the shelves are stacked with things that will trap, poison, gas or electronically zap practically any unwanted creature.

Unfortunately for Gerry, there were no new 'wonder' devices on the shelves. He'd tried the dynamite-shaped sticks that you light and leave in the tunnel, and the sonic devices which claimed to be so ear-piercing they would send the poor mammals running in the opposite direction. Poisons have never appealed to either of us, so those were out. The only option left was trapping. As soon as we got back, he went down and assessed the ground, working out the position of the tunnels, and the best place to catch his prey. The killer devices were positioned and cocked for action, and a restless night of anticipation followed.

In the morning, Gerry couldn't wait to get down there and see the result of his labours. He wasn't disappointed – two tiny black creatures with pin-head eyes and disproportionately large feet had been caught in the act. He was triumphant. Moles 0, Gerry Toms 2.

But the battle doesn't end there. Gerry's police and Territorial Army training has taught him to expect the unexpected, so he won't rest for a good while yet. His favourite areas will be inspected every day for signs of retaliation from the enemy. Sneaky beggars, those moles, you know.

I've personally got nothing against moles – but then, they've never damaged crops I've grown, nor ventured into my flowerbeds. And I've never been a lover of a carefully mown sward of characterless green grass.

But if you're a gardener or farmer really bothered by moles you'll know the damage they can cause to growing plants. Each creature consumes between 70 per cent and 100 per cent of its body weight in food each day, burrowing its way through metres of earth in the search for sustenance. On the one hand, they feed primarily on the kind of insects gardeners regard as pests, but they also eat useful earthworms and other invertebrates which help to aerate the soil. I was amazed to learn that they can move their own weight in soil in just one minute, and each tunnel can stretch for 1,000m or more.

Barriers are supposed to deter them. They don't like compacted or stony soil, and some people recommend digging a trench around vulnerable areas and filling it with chicken wire or stone. Others say noise or vibration act as deterrents. It's often suggested that wine bottles buried in the soil will put the moles off as the wind blows along the top of the necks and makes a whistling sound – but somehow I doubt that one really works.

Moles don't like strong smells, and some people swear by a strong solution of Jeyes fluid poured down a hole, about one part water to 20 parts of the product.

If you live somewhere not overlooked by neighbours, you might fancy trying the even cheaper, no-mixing-involved, human urine method. Apparently, moles dislike the smell even more than that of Jeyes fluid, but Gerry hasn't put this one to the test yet. You can be sure I'll let you know if he does.

October

There have been so many men that I sometimes forget all their names. I know there was a John, I think there was a Terry, and maybe a Paul and an Ian, and there was definitely an Andrew – but some names just escape me altogether. I think I'd have been better off giving them numbers, quite honestly.

Glyn was particularly nice, and was around for quite a while, so I got to know him quite well. We used to have long conversations, and he seemed to understand my feelings. Some of them were pleasant enough, but just did what they had to do and left. But my favourite gentleman caller, without a doubt, was Eugene – the one who did what none of the others could do for me: he fixed my phone line. And, fingers crossed, it looks like he's finally done the trick.

I've been living here in our 'rural idyll' for almost four years now and for the first time I have a telephone service which resembles those enjoyed by the majority of other households – the kind that most people take for granted. As you can imagine, I'm over-joyed. I was on the point of offering to have Eugene's babies.

I can now make calls with a degree of confidence that the line won't drop out at some point during the conversation, leaving the person on the other end talking to themselves, and then assuming I've put the phone down.

I'm hoping that I'll be able to delete the BT fault line number from my mobile phone, and forget all about listening to recorded messages, choosing options, and then going through the whole ridiculous process of explaining the nature of our long-running, intermittent fault. I'll try to erase from my memory the debilitating experience of assur-ing the BT person that it's not the actual phone but the line – so there's no point in me unplugging it from the socket and trying it in other extensions. And I'll do my best to remove all thoughts of waiting while the fault person tests my land line – only to find, low and behold – that it's working again.

It's fantastic to be able to send and receive e-mails and surf the internet for work or pleasure – not when the system lets me, but whenever I feel like it. Gerry and I don't miss out on time-sensitive offers of work, and friends and relatives can keep in touch with us just as easily as they do with other folk.

It's been a good six weeks or so since I had my rant about the phone line in this column. It certainly jump-started the process. Things started to happen rapidly, with a BT man (now what was *his* name?) on the doorstep within hours of the *Western Mail* hitting the streets. Two additional telegraph poles were erected in one of our bottom fields and something else done to the line but, despite all being well for a few days, the fault reappeared.

Back to square one. Another engineer was ordered. He left a card saying he had fixed the line, but I soon proved him wrong. Eventually, after making probably my most Victor Meldrew-ish call to the fault line, my knight in shining armour – or, rather, hard hat and flourescent waterproof jacket – turned up.

He and his colleague began major surgery on the line, and, within a few hours, the fault was fixed. What's more, as an added bonus, my internet speed shot up from a dismal 28kbps to a supersonic 44! Okay, so it's still not the 56kbps that many people are used to, but it's made a world of difference to me.

They even did a broadband test while they were here and, although they found out that we won't be able to get it, it seems that we will in less than two years, so there's some hope. In the mean time, however, I'm just really content with what I've got. I may not be racing down the internet super-highway, but I'm tootling along at a respectable pace.

November

The word 'domesticity' was never mentioned in the same breath as my name. I can't pretend I've ever been one for doing things at home, and I've always clung to the excuse that full-time workers should do everything possible to support the convenience food industry.

I've managed to get by. I did compulsory cookery lessons at school, and learned enough to be able to make cheese and potato pie. And, probably by osmosis, I picked up from my mum the trick of making gravy without using Bisto granules.

All was well until we bought an old farmhouse with an Aga – a curious, hulking beast with a metal shell of the most hideous Ford Anglia blue. Friends – green with envy, for some reason – had told me it was simplicity itself. It was all a question of getting used to it.

They lied. They said it was perfect for roasting meat: well, yes – as long as you can remember to take the joint out. The trouble is, with an outdoor flue, there are absolutely no cooking smells in the kitchen. The only time you twig is when you're working outside, probably up to your knees in some mucky job, and the unmistakeable whiff of burning wafts your way.

If the meat is in the roasting oven, you've little chance of rescuing anything. If, on the other hand, it's in the simmering one, chances are it'll still be edible, but will have given up looking like the nice topside joint you started cooking. It's most likely to have taken on the consistency of stewed steak. We've developed quite a taste for stewed steak in our house – just as well, as my record for keeping a joint in the oven now stands at two-and-a-half days.

Our chimney is busier than the local crematorium. So far I've successfully destroyed not just joints, but chops, sausages, pies, and even whole chickens. The emerging results are so charred beyond recognition that not even the wild farm cats will cast a second glance.

Cakes are just as hazardous. In my teens I developed the knack for impressive Victoria sponges, and got quite good at it. Those skills would translate quite easily to the Aga, you'd have thought. Not a chance. First, the narrowness of the oven meant that I couldn't put two sandwich tins side by side – so one cooked (or burned) faster than the other. When I tried swapping them round halfway through, they sank in the middle, or at best rose to biscuit-height. I added baking powder. Big mistake. Opening the oven, the cakes had disappeared, leaving empty tins. They rose so much, the tops stuck to the roof of the oven, and the tins dropped back onto the shelf.

The first Christmas, the turkey took so long to cook, we sat down to 'lunch' at 6.30 p.m.; the following year's was so 'well done', it took till Boxing Day to finish chewing the damned thing. With our third Christmas approaching, I booked myself on a Christmas cooking demonstration at the Aga shop.

The demonstrator was, as you would expect, confident and efficient, but also offered quite a few shortcuts (frozen pastry, cooked chestnuts) to easing the stress of the Big Day. Oh, but so much juggling of pots and pans, tins and trays! Put the tray on the top shelf, move it down to the bottom when the veg is ready, shake this, baste that ... too much to think about. And all that after saying the key to cooking on Christmas Day was to relax! Mind you, she also recommended cooking with a bottle of champagne at hand. Now *that* idea appealed to me! Who cares about Christmas dinner?

December

Back in the days when I was a proper journalist, I used to travel about quite a lot. As a showbiz writer, I had to interview all the top celebrities, which usually meant trekking back and forth across London, attending previews of major new TV series, and eating and drinking far too much at sumptuous press receptions.

It wasn't unusual for me to be catching the train to Paddington two or three times a week. I would line up on the platform in Cardiff alongside the hoards of grey-faced, Monday-to-Friday commuters, and I knew exactly where to stand to be within inches of the door when the train arrived. Once on board, I would make my way to my favourite seat (the double one at the back of the carriage, so that I didn't have to sit opposite anyone or play footsie with a stranger's briefcase under the table), read my *Western Mail*, take a few swigs of coffee, and fall asleep until Swindon. The return journey would be pretty much the same, with the bit in the middle a kind of a hectic, whistle-stop blur by the end of the day.

All a long time ago. Often it seems like a lifetime away. Aside from the travelling, I really enjoyed myself at the time, but I doubt whether I'd have the stamina to do it all these days.

And would I really want to? I had to go to London for a couple of business meetings last week, and I'd forgotten how much hassle it all was – and how bad that city smells. Working from home most of the time, I tend to forget the people stuck on their hamster treadmills, forced to do the same thing, day in, day out.

Sitting on the train in a smart business suit – with full make-up and clean hair – was something of a novelty for me. I felt a bit of a fraud and, looking round, I wondered whether anyone could have guessed what my life was really like. One look at my rough hands, ingrained with dirt, might have given them a clue. Normally at that time of the morning, I would have been wearing a fleece with a waterproof jacket on top, water-proof elasticated trousers, a big hat, fishermen's socks and wellies.

The day went really well: the meetings were a success, and I treated myself to a bit of shopping amid the dazzling Oxford Street Christmas lights. Untroubled by the thought of animal feeding times (Gerry took a day off work, bless him), I strolled around the sweet-smelling department stores, tried on some glamorous clothes, and snapped up a bargain pair of leather boots. Then I shook off the stresses and strains of the day with a few drinks in very convivial company. On the downside, when I got home I had a barney with Gerry because I fell asleep on the train and forgot to ring to say I was going to be late. But, being the nice chap he is, he forgave me – eventually.

The next morning, I was Cinderella again, minus the shiny shoes and back in the muddy wellies, driving my pumpkin Land Rover. Back down to earth in the truest sense. As the animals waiting for their food gave me a welcoming chorus, I sniffed the air, the crisp, clean air and paused for a while to watch a sparrowhawk swooping down into the wood. Giving the pigs their usual scratch behind the ears, I wondered when my next trip to the big city might be. Probably not for a long time.

And then I started to think about all those people standing on the platform, waiting for the train; waiting to go back to a noisy, dirty place, where unsmiling people push past you in the street and car fumes burn the back of your throat.

Then I remembered how lucky I really am. At least I can step into their world whenever I like. They, on the other hand, probably haven't got much choice.

INDEX